CAUSE!

A BUSINESS STRATEGY FOR STANDING OUT IN A SEA OF SAMENESS

JACKIE AND KEVIN FREIBERG
AUTHORS OF INTERNATIONAL BEST SELLER NUTS!

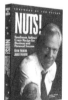     

For multiple copies and bulk orders, please contact our office
T: 619.624.9691 E: info@freibergs.com

Published by freibergs.com, a San Diego Consulting Group, Inc. company.
Copyright © 2015 San Diego Consulting Group, Inc.

ISBN: 978-0-692-58666-2

Designed by Emma Strong, San Diego, California

DEDICATION:

To everyone who wants to be a part of a winning story. A story about making your corner of the world better. If you can dream it, we invite you to do it. This book is your "how to" on what it means to join and invest in companies that are committed to helping you achieve your dreams, have a positive social impact and make a difference.

QR CODES

If you are unfamiliar with them, a QR Code or Quick Response Code is a two dimensional barcode that can be read using smartphone applications and dedicated QR reading devices. A QR code links directly to video, emails, websites, phone numbers, text and more.

You will find many QR codes in this book; so let's get started! Go to the App Store and download a QR reader. There are many to choose from, here are a few options:

Barcode Scanner
Zapper
NeoReader
Kaywa

freibergs.com

WE WANT TO HEAR FROM YOU AT KEVINANDJACKIE@FREIBERGS.COM

jackiefreiberg   kevinfreiberg

drjackiefreiberg

TABLE OF CONTENTS

LETTER FROM THE AUTHORS

We have been writing about **best places, where the best people can do their best work, to make the world better,** since the early 1990s, before it was cool to be a **best place**. Now, 30 years into our journey we have come across another best place—a very grounded company called National Life Group, recently recognized as #19 out of 85 in the LIMRA 2014 U.S. Retail Life Insurance Sales Survey. National Life is a company that is serious about culture, cause, and LOVE (Living Our Values Every day).

We wrote this book for a couple of reasons.

First, we believe that cause drives culture. And defining the business as a cause will inspire a movement. These are the keys to awakening peoples' passion, creating innovative solutions for all people, attracting the best talent, restoring dreams, creating brand enthusiasts, and ultimately changing an industry.

Second, we are fired up about companies that are committed to empowering and enabling all employees to engage in work that matters.

This book is a reminder of what it means to be a part of something special…a company grounded in LOVE and a community of people who are committed to a cause that makes the world better.

KEVIN AND JACKIE FREIBERG

The dogmas of the quiet past are inadequate to the stormy present. The occasion is piled high with difficulty, and we must rise—with the occasion.

Abraham Lincoln
Annual Message to Congress, 1862

GIVE HISTORY A SHOVE

On May 25, 1961, President John F. Kennedy announced before a special joint session of Congress the dramatic and ambitious goal of putting an American on the moon and bringing him home safely before the end of the decade.

The dream was bold and audacious, but it galvanized a nation and launched a movement. That one simple, yet extraordinary, declaration ignited the entire U.S. scientific community along with an army of government officials and private sector entrepreneurs.

Thousands of people from thousands of places worked long hours making personal and professional sacrifices to bring thousands of puzzle pieces together. It was one of the greatest mobilizations of resources and manpower in history!

What was so compelling about the vision?

Why were the people involved so committed?

Kennedy invited us into a cause. He asked us to be part of something BIGGER, to bring our gifts and talents to solve a problem that really mattered. His challenge appealed to our spirit of adventure. Space revolutionaries were determined to give history a shove by doing what no one had ever done before.

The cause appealed to our sense of pride. In the Cold War Era, the thought of the Soviets beating us to the moon was unbearable and no one wanted to let our country down.

For the rest of the world, it was the thrill of opening new doors. Not only would a successful moon landing open up a new frontier for humankind, it would also inevitably spawn new innovations.

After Kennedy's assassination, as America went through the turmoil of the Vietnam War, the civil rights movement, and more assassinations, the Apollo program seemed to symbolize the ingenuity and entrepreneurial spirit of our people; it reminded us of the America we wanted to be.

Despite skeptics who said it couldn't be done, on July 20, 1969, over a half a billion people around the world watched as Neil Armstrong took a small step for himself and a giant step for mankind.

> *A critical mass of innovators and technologists opened their minds, tapped into the intellectual capital of the nation, and rose to the occasion.*

It was a stunning achievement that represented the best of human ingenuity and demonstrated the heights to which the human spirit can rise when inspired by a noble, heroic cause.

It is said that we only knew approximately 15 percent of what we needed to know to accomplish this goal when Kennedy made the commitment. Yet, somehow, a critical mass of innovators and technologists opened their minds, tapped into the intellectual capital of the nation, and rose to the occasion.

Imagination is the beginning of creation.

You imagine what you desire, you will what you
imagine and at last you create what you will.

George Bernard Shaw
Man and Superman

WHAT IF?

What if you could be a part of a team determined to give history a shove, rise to the occasion, and achieve great things?

What if you could be a part of a team that had a burning passion to create not just a company but a legacy that would live on long after you've left the scene?

What if you could be a part of a business that earns the love and respect of family, friends, and colleagues? A business committed to making a profit while making a difference? A business admired by clients and envied by competitors?

What if this business had a culture that is bound by love instead of driven by fear? A culture where leaders are hard-working servants who mentor and inspire rather than manipulate and control. What if you could create a place that is as human as the human beings who work there, a place where people feel valued, add value, and live their values, not because they have to but because they want to?

What if potential team members and partners beat a path to the door because they knew the business excelled at equipping people for success? They could sense the collaboration and camaraderie among people who share the same passion and belong to something bigger—people who go home at the end of the day physically tired but emotionally charged because they are engaged in a heroic cause that inspires them.

What if you could create a company that cares about the wellness and well-being of its customers and sees its customers as real people with real families and real dreams, not just market segments, prospects, and sales quotas? What if this business treated its customers with a spirit of hospitality, the kind you encounter when people anticipate your needs, are genuinely glad to see you, and consider it a privilege to serve you? What if you created a business that focused on enriching lives, not just pushing products? Think of a business that could never knowingly manipulate, mislead, or mistreat its "customers and partners."

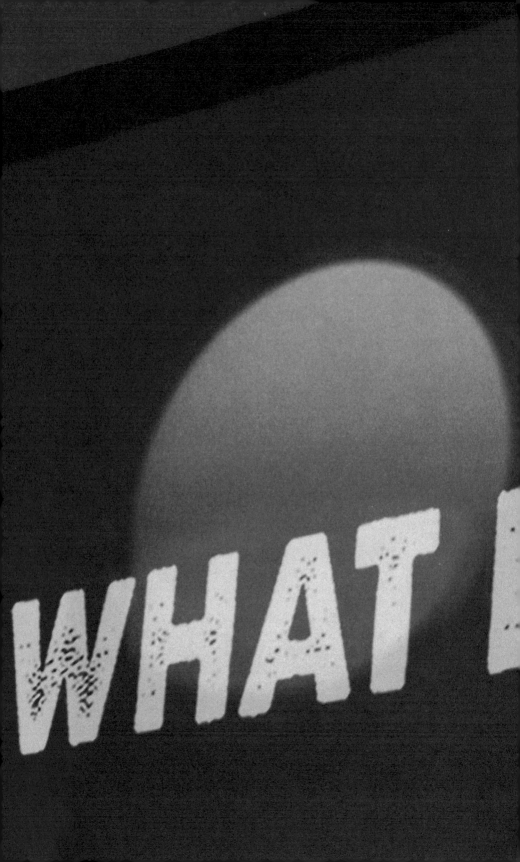

What if this company led the charge for a more sustainable future, or genuinely respects the environment? What if this business was a force for GOOD in the world because it enriches the lives of EVERYONE it touches.

What if this company didn't think of itself as just a business, but rather as a community of like-minded individuals pooling talents to make good on a promise? What if you could create not just a company, but a movement that has the power to leverage free enterprise to bring peace of mind and financial well-being to life for those you serve?

What if this wasn't a utopian dream? What if you could actually be a part of a company like this? What if you weren't just colleagues at work but rather friends committed to a cause?

THIS must be the vision for any company that wants to turn employees into ambassadors, partners into enthusiasts, and customers into advocates. These companies must turn "What if?" into "What is!"

At a 2015 town hall meeting, Mehran Assadi, President and CEO of National Life, opened the event with this:

We are a mission-driven company, as such we are in good company. Apple is in business to enrich lives, Google to organize the world's information, Southwest Airlines is in business to democratize the skies. We are creating peace of mind for everyone we touch."

He went on to say, "We must recruit to a winning story—if you want to dream it and do it then come to National Life—we are Do Gooders."

WHO IS TURNING "WHAT IF?" TO "WHAT IS!"?

Since our first book, *NUTS! Southwest Airlines' Crazy Recipe for Business and Personal Success,* became an international best seller, it has not been unusual for leaders to ask us to write their company story, too.

However, when you make your living telling stories, there better be a phenomenal story to tell. We seldom say "yes" because that rare blend of the right stuff that truly does make the world better is, well…rare.

National Life Group was founded on Servant Leadership principles, on one man's desire to make life better for people in rural New England. And the company has stayed grounded in these principles for over 167 years.

Even today, as Wall Street and the big guys try to exploit so many small-to-mid-size companies, National Life is as Main Street USA today as it was when it started. Like the crisp Vermont morning air, we found that refreshing.

At National Life we've discovered a community of people who are die-hard about advancing financial literacy, paving the way for free enterprise and entrepreneurship, helping people realize the American Dream, and delivering on promises. From what we've learned, National Life is democratizing financial services for everyone interested in a better future.

This book is a wake-up call to anyone who doubts the significance of their contribution. When you realize your profession matters and your work enriches lives, your work takes on more meaning and significance. Your job becomes a calling and your contributions give rise to a movement.

Regardless of what you do or where you work, we hope this book and the stories housed within it will inspire you, too, to Do Good on Main Street, on Wall Street, and on your street.

IT'S YOUR TURN TO GIVE HISTORY A SHOVE AND RISE TO SUCH AN OCCASION.

WHO ARE WE?
WHY DO WE EXIST?
WHAT'S NOBLE
AND HEROIC ABOUT
WHAT WE DO?

PART 1
THE ROI OF CAUSE
THE NEW DRIVING FORCE FOR BUSINESS SUCCESS

National Life might be one of America's best-kept secrets, but it's a secret that is giving history a shove. And National Life happens to be in good company.

There is an undeniable wave cresting. The wave is a new breed of companies that are purpose-driven and cause-oriented. They are forward-thinking and intentional about doing good, connecting dreams to opportunities, and launching movements that make the world better. Their success and confidence come from defining their business as a cause.

Their confidence attracts and unleashes talent, accelerates innovation, strengthens brand reputation, moves markets, allows the organization to move with speed and agility, stimulates investments, and creates long-term growth.

Companies that are committed to solving problems that matter and dedicated to creating a better world for all stakeholders (employees, customers, vendors, and community) are almost always cause-oriented. That is, they are committed to making a profit while making a difference. These companies have answered four critical questions:

Who are we? Why do we exist? What's noble and heroic about what we do? In terms of meaningful impact on the world, if we were gone tomorrow why would we be missed?

The answers to these questions grow confidence, guide behavior, drive strategy, transcend leaders, and endure over time. They give everyone in the organization a reason to come to work every day.

TURNS OUT THAT NOT ONLY
IS "DOING GOOD"
A MORAL IMPERATIVE,
IT'S GOOD FOR BUSINESS.

There is a strong correlation between a noble, heroic cause and the confidence necessary to build and sustain a successful enterprise. Deloitte's Core Beliefs & Culture survey shows that cause-oriented firms are more confident in their forecasts for future growth. And so they tend to invest heavily in new initiatives and new technologies or expand into new markets that lead to long-term growth.

The report—based on a survey of 1,053 executives and employees with full-time jobs in organizations with over 100 employees—found that 82 percent of respondents (executives and employees) who work for an organization with a strong sense of purpose say they are confident that their organization will grow, compared to 48 percent of those whose organizations do not have a strong sense of purpose.

Need a business case for defining the business as a cause? Check out the following pages; the ROI (Return on Investment) is hard to ignore.

It turns out that not only is "doing good" a moral imperative, it's good for business.

GREATER LONG-TERM INVESTMENT

According to the Deloitte Core Beliefs & Culture survey, people who work for cause-oriented companies believe their company will heavily reinvest.

Consider the following investment differences between firms with a strong sense of purpose and those without:

- New technologies: 38% vs. 19%
- Expanding into new markets: 31% vs. 21%
- Forming new strategic partnerships: 31% vs. 18%
- Developing new products and services: 27% vs. 17%
- Employee development and training: 25% vs. 11%
- Leadership development: 23% vs. 11%

Confident, forward-thinking, business leaders drive innovation, mold and maintain company culture, invest in technology, explore new relationships, and maximize the use of resources strategically. This makes sense. Everyone knows that reinvesting is crucial to a company's continued growth and success. Yet, the companies driven by a cause lean into this more. Why?

Changing the world is not for the faint of heart. It's for people crazy enough to step out of the routine and into the breach to have a positive impact.

They carry a courage that makes others question their sanity and a focus that inspires other like-minded change makers to follow.

When there is a cause worth fighting for and a problem worth solving, the passion and the compelling business case for reinvesting is stronger.

The idea is that when we believe what we are doing is so meaningful and so important then we naturally believe that we can't afford NOT to reinvest.

General Electric's (GE) passion for making a profit while making a difference was built around its cause: Ecomagination. The aim of the cause is to invest in clean technology research and development, introduce green products to customers, and reduce GE's greenhouse gas emissions.

Leveraging the power of crowdsourcing, GE engaged its entire workforce in developing Ecomagination. Employees collaborated to design new products and new ways to cut energy use. The results ranged from revamping GE manufacturing plants and creating more efficient routes for GE trucks to rolling out new consumer products like compact fluorescent lights.

GE employees gained new skills, motivation, and a sense of pride in the company from doing something good for the environment. Meanwhile, GE doubled its investment in and revenue from green technologies.

ATTRACT "IMPACT" TALENT.

When your business is tied to a noble, heroic cause—a movement to make the world better— people will beat a path to your door. But not just any people. Not wannabes, but change makers. People who are moved by and connected to the purpose, people who also see their work as a calling and a crusade.

Changing the world is not for the faint of heart. It's for people crazy enough to step out of the routine and into the breach to have a positive impact. They carry a courage that makes others question their sanity and a focus that inspires other like-minded change makers to follow.

Net Impact, a nonprofit membership organization for students and professionals interested in using business skills in support of various social and environmental causes, asked students and workers what factors were essential to their happiness. The Talent Report shows that after marriage, children, and financial security, having a job "where I can have an impact" is most important.

A majority of students (65 percent) expect to make a positive social or environmental difference in the world within six years of joining the workforce Furthermore, 58 percent said they would take a 15 percent pay cut to get this kind of opportunity.

WE MAKE A LIVING BY WHAT WE GET, BUT WE MAKE A LIFE BY WHAT WE GIVE

WINSTON CHURCHILL

CHECK OUT THE FINDINGS.

All other things being equal, I would take a 15% pay cut…

- 83%…for a job that makes a social or environmental impact
- 88%…to work for an organization with values like my own
- 71%…to work for a company committed to CSR (Corporate Social Responsibility)

When your company offers something that's more purposeful than just a job with a paycheck, you win.

WHAT ABOUT PROFESSIONALS CURRENTLY EMPLOYED?

A little more than half (55 percent) say they are currently in a job where they can make a social or environmental impact on the world. And they are more satisfied by a ratio of 2:1. For example, 49 percent report high satisfaction levels, compared to just 24 percent of those who do not have impact opportunities at work.

More firms today (40,000) are publishing CSR (Corporate Social Responsibility) reports to show prospective employees that they have a triple bottom line (people, planet, profit) and that they can have an impact.

IT consulting company Capgemini understands the power of a cause in attracting impact talent. Rather than offer a t-shirt or CPS (cheap plastic stuff) to individuals who completed a 30-minute recruiting survey, Capgemini offered to fund a week of schooling for a needy child in India.

The response was huge. Approximately 10,000 people completed the survey and submitted resumés. From those respondents, Capgemini found 2,000 job candidates who were a fit and ultimately hired 800 people. The entire exercise also funded 10,000 weeks of education for Indian children.

Is your job big enough for your spirit?

CAUSE ELEVATES EMPLOYEE ENGAGEMENT

Employees want more than a paycheck. They want a sense of pride and fulfillment from their work. And, they don't want to check their values at the door when they come to work; they want a company whose values match their own.

As we will argue, when the business becomes a cause what follows is a movement and people OPT-IN to movements.

WHEN THE BUSINESS BECOMES
A CAUSE WHAT FOLLOWS
IS A MOVEMENT AND PEOPLE
OPT-IN TO MOVEMENTS

Employees are most passionate and engaged when they are fighting for a cause that is tied to their own deep-seated values—when work is an opportunity to invest themselves in issues that are important to them. This makes work a natural and impactful expression of who they are. Essentially, it helps them answer two very important questions:

DO I BELONG HERE? IS THERE CONGRUENCE BETWEEN WHAT THE ORGANIZATION STANDS FOR AND WHAT I STAND FOR?

The answers are telling. With congruence something very powerful happens. People bring more of themselves to work. They bring their best selves.

What makes people spiritually, emotionally, and physically sick? What makes them tired? What makes them empty or depressed, not engaged? A life that is incongruent. Without congruence, well-being and engagement go out the door.

Engaged people are more open to new information, more productive, more adaptive, and more willing to go the extra mile. Moreover, engaged people are all in; they take the initiative to change their work environments in order to stay engaged.

IBM found this to be true with the launch and growth of its Corporate Service Corps (CSC) plan. The program operates like a corporate version of the Peace Corps where IBMers bring their skills and experience in project management, strategic planning, marketing, or engineering to an entrepreneurial company based in a developing country. Think Brazil, China, Ghana, India, Malaysia, Romania, and South Africa, to name a few.

IBM launched Corporate Service Corps (CSC) as an integral part of a larger effort to help IBMers think and act like global leaders. By working and living in one of these emerging markets, IBMers develop sensitivity to new cultures, encounter different people with disparate needs and expectations, and become global citizens.

AS AN EMPLOYER THAT WANTS TO HAVE AN IMPACT IN THE WORLD, IBM'S CSC PAVES THE WAY FOR WANNABES TO BECOME CHANGE MAKERS.

This is just one example of doing good for yourself by doing good for others. IBM builds a global leadership mentality among its people, and its people enrich lives and raise the tide for entire countries by expanding the competencies and skills of local entrepreneurs.

CORPORATE
CULTURE
MATTERS

CAUSE STRENGTHENS CULTURE.

Costco co-founder Jim Sinegal said that when it comes to growing and sustaining a business, "Culture is not the most important thing—it's the only thing." Sinegal's comment reflects what some of the most successful CEOs in the world have in common: a fanatical focus on culture.

Entrepreneur magazine quoted Richard Branson, Virgin Group's founder, as saying: "Culture is one of the most underappreciated essentials in business. No matter how visionary, brilliant, and far-reaching a leader's strategy might be, it can all come undone if it is not fully supported by a strong and spirited corporate culture."

As the newly appointed CEO of National Life, Mehran Assadi sensed the value of culture and cause. In an effort to stand out in an industry recognized as a sea of sameness and to increase competiveness, Assadi made culture and cause strategic priorities. Five years later, National Life is changed. New talent wants in, employees and agents are more engaged, customers are loyal, and the industry is taking notice as National Life celebrates double-digit growth in annuities and life insurance.

Herb Kelleher, Southwest Airlines' iconic founder, will tell you that the most important committee at Southwest is the Culture Committee—a cross functional team of over 100 people who are charged with keeping the culture alive and strong.

It was over 25 years ago that we learned cause drives culture. In the early 70s Southwest Airlines fought 43 judicial and administrative proceedings, all the way to the U.S. Supreme Court, for the right to fly. Three major carriers, Braniff, Continental, and Texas International colluded to squash the little upstart before it could legitimately get one plane in the air. These hard-fought battles gave birth to a warrior spirit. Today, this spirit remains an essential part of the Southwest culture and a major contributor to one of the most productive workforces in the world, unprecedented profitability, and industry differentiation.

The Deloitte Core Beliefs & Culture survey indicates that organizations with a compelling cause are more likely to have strong corporate cultures than those that don't.

CAUSE
DRIVES
CULTURE

Companies with a compelling cause and strong corporate culture are:

- 83% more likely to embrace diversity and different options
- 80% more likely to encourage employees to innovate
- 79% more likely to encourage people to develop new business growth opportunities
- 74% more likely to provide tools for employees to reach their full potential
- 73% more likely to have leaders who seek out the opinions/ideas of others

"The most important thing you can do as a leader is create an environment where everyone knows that what they do makes a difference." That's from David Novak, chairman of Yum! Brands, parent company of Pizza Hut, Taco Bell, and KFC.

Novak knows that a noble, heroic cause has the power to create a culture where people are encouraged, appreciated, and willing to achieve extraordinary results.

Still not convinced? Go study the stories of USAA, Whole Foods, Medtronic, and Patagonia. Each of these companies has a thick, identifiable culture that saturates the entire organization. All have cultures that are driven by a cause.

CAUSE ELEVATES CUSTOMER ENGAGEMENT.

Consumer preferences are shifting. It's no longer enough to sell a product or service that works. Consumers expect meaningful social impact. In the future, if you can't demonstrate that you are legitimately doing something to make the world better, you won't have a business. Check out the following studies.

Edelman's 2014 Trust Barometer study revealed that 92 percent of consumers want to do business with companies that share their concerns (e.g., economic development, the environment, human rights, poverty, and hunger) and 40 percent of consumers don't think brands are doing enough to demonstrate their beliefs in helping the world.

The Reputation Institute's 2013 Survey showed that while 73 percent of consumers are willing to recommend companies that stand for something meaningful, only 5 percent believe that companies actually deliver on their promises.

Consider the results from a 2013 survey done by marketing agency Good.Must. Grow: 30 percent of those surveyed said that they expect to increase the amount of goods and services they buy from socially-responsible companies in the next year (previously it was 18 percent).

Among consumers ages 40-44, 50% will pay more for products associated with a cause.

And millennials are even more likely to spend more with companies that give back.

Does your business give back? Are you engaging consumers by telling your story?

The Nielsen Global Survey on Corporate Social Responsibility surveyed more than 29,000 respondents in 58 countries. Among consumers ages 40–44, 50 percent said they would pay more for products associated with a cause (up from 38 percent two years ago). The millennials are even more likely to spend more with companies that give back.

A study by public relations and marketing firm Cone Communications and Echo Research said 90 percent of shoppers worldwide are likely to switch to brands that support a good cause, given similar price and quality. Also, 90 percent of the 10,000 shoppers surveyed would boycott companies if they found the firms were negligent or guilty of irresponsible business practices.

Is your business making the world better?

The question of social entrepreneurship and social responsibility is a key topic in Davos, Switzerland at the World Economic Forum's annual meeting, where global business leaders wrestle each year with the issue of public distrust and the imperative for companies to do good for themselves while doing good for the world.

Toilet paper from Seventh Generation. Shoes from TOMS. Artisan products from Sevenly. Coats from Patagonia. Ice cream from Ben & Jerry's. There will always be some market segment that religiously buys goods from socially responsible companies.

BUT IF YOU THINK THEY ARE OUT ON THE FRINGE, THINK AGAIN. MORE AND MORE OF THESE SOCIALLY CONSCIOUS BUYERS REPRESENT CENTER STAGE.

The market is hungry for something genuine to believe in.

STRONGER FINANCIAL PERFORMANCE

There is a cause-and-effect relationship between a firm's ability to serve a higher cause, to do good, and its financial performance.

Procter & Gamble's former Chief Marketing Officer, Jim Stengel, in concert with Millward Brown Optimor, the second largest marketing research firm next to Nielsen, conducted an unprecedented, ten-year growth study utilizing a global database of more than 50,000 brands.

The brands that built the deepest relationships with customers while achieving the greatest financial growth from 2001–2011 were called the Stengel 50.

Here's what the Stengel 50 had in common. They were built on an ideal of improving lives and making the world better in some way, irrespective of size and category.

They defined "ideal" as the higher-order benefit a brand or a business gives to the world. They found that this cause was both a source of inspiration externally among customers as well as a compass for internal decision making.

THE RESULTS WERE IMPRESSIVE:

- The Stengel 50 grew three times faster than their competitors.
- The Stengel 50 outperformed the S&P 500 by almost 400 percent over the same 10 years.

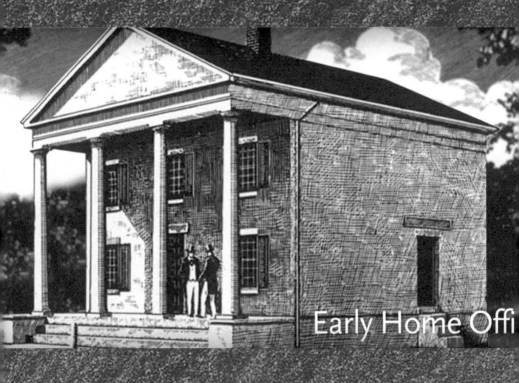

Early Home Offi

PART 2

NATIONAL LIFE
NOT JUST A COMPANY—A CAUSE

I n all that we have learned, it is clear that for over 167 years the people of National Life have been relentless about a cause—making promises, keeping promises, and bringing assurance, peace of mind, and financial well-being to those they serve.

In 1848, when National Life Insurance Co. was founded there were just 30 states, construction of the Washington Monument was just beginning, James Polk was President, and word of the California Gold Rush was spreading.

A look back in time suggests that National Life has been a valued partner to the history makers of this country. When young men rushed to California to make their fortunes in the Gold Rush, quite a few carried a National Life policy in their back pocket. When U.S. soldiers went into battle during the Civil War and the World Wars, National Life provided the peace of mind families needed back at home. National Life insured passengers on the Titanic and the Hindenburg. And in 1850, when virtually no women were insured in America, National Life issued policy #43 on Laura Ann Peaslee Webster.

Throughout America's iconic past the people of National Life have been committed to making good on every promise in a noble effort to provide the trusted assurance of an even brighter future.

EVEN THOUGH INDUSTRY SALES ARE FLAT, NATIONAL LIFE SALES SOAR.

According to CEO Mehran Assadi,

"Our leaders are different than they were just 6 years ago. We are no longer leading through command and control. Leadership is about finding joy in serving others. Leadership is not a right; it is a gift and today, more so than ever, we must earn the privilege to lead."

Fast forward to 2015 and National Life still has many virtues to tout: financial strength, ratings, history, responsible investment practices, and products. Are these virtues exclusive to National Life? No, some of their competitors have similar bragging rights.

SO WHAT SETS NATIONAL LIFE APART?

Relationships. Personal relationships. Authentic relationships. Lasting relationships.

And at the heart of every relationship is trust…trust that when life happens, National Life will come through.

That trust is earned every day. It is not good enough that they have been delivering on their promises since 1848. Today's new policy holders must believe that National Life will be here for them—tomorrow, and for many, many tomorrows in the future. How? By building trust one relationship, one call, one solution at a time. When a policy holder calls, they talk to a real person who listens and responds through LOVE (the practice of "Living Our Values Every day"). And living their values every day has withstood the test of time; National Life was established in 1848 and today it is the third oldest mutually held life insurance company in the United States.

The company is committed to the practice of Servant Leadership and makes a concerted effort to ensure that every person who works for or with National Life lives its Servant Leadership tenets.

The tenets were created for employees by employees. Every year the company conducts an all employee survey, asking for anonymous feedback regarding goals, recognition, and trust. Feedback is collected and shared with employees to ensure transparency. Trends are identified and issues are given to working groups to improve. The practice of Servant Leadership has made a difference for employees and customers alike.

Here are a few comments from some policy owners who have been personally touched by the actions of National Life people practicing Servant Leadership and living their values every day:

> *Words are inadequate to express my appreciation and gratitude to you for the way you helped me out recently. I can only hope that National Life understands what a true gem they have in you.*

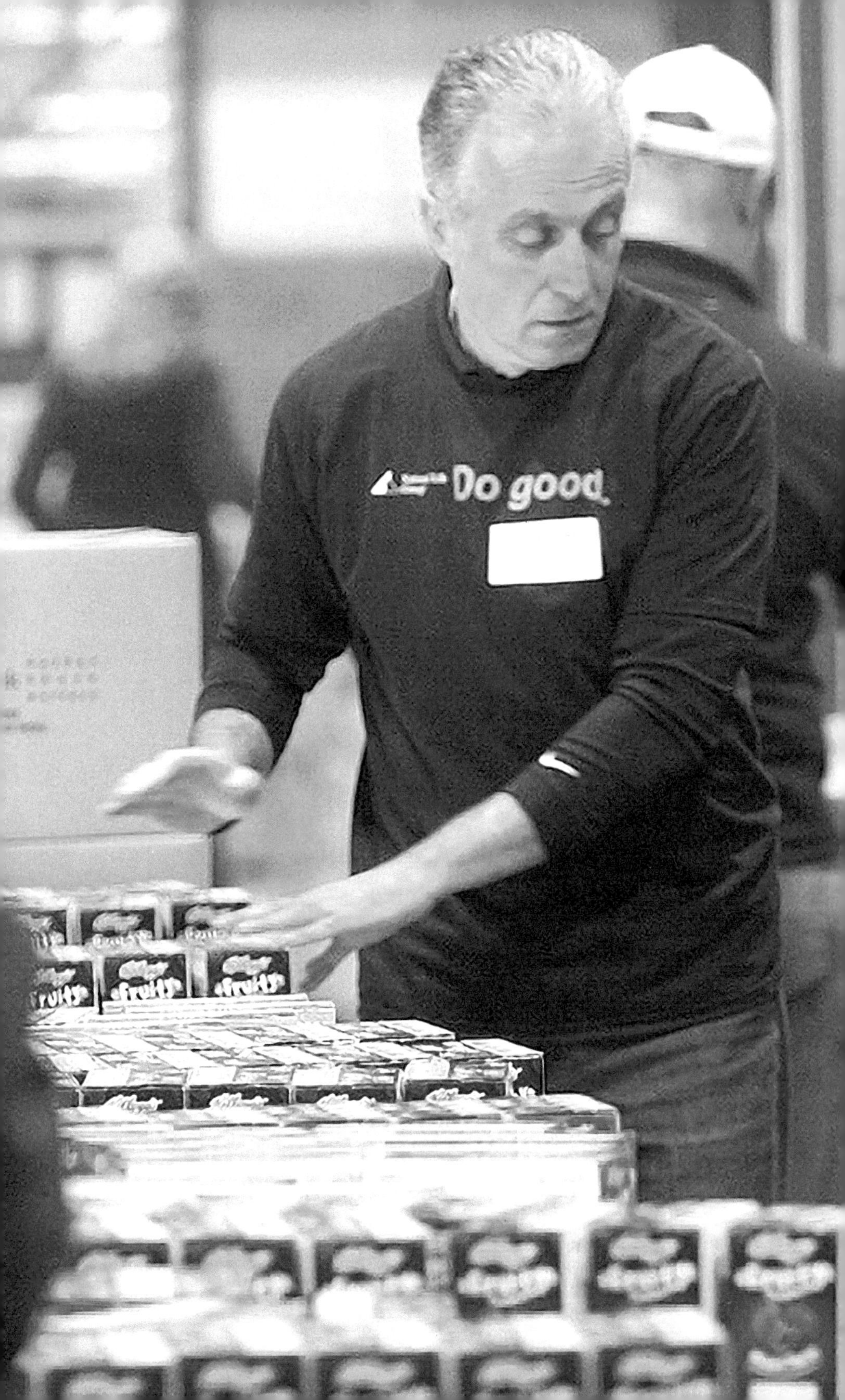
Do good

I am proud to tell your company how patiently, warmly, and most knowledgeably and competently you answered all my concerns. Thank you for working with me, even when I was quite upset, not stopping, proactively, until you had resolved all my issues and made me feel comfortable with how things were going and I had a full understanding of the issues that needed to be resolved...which, with your help, were successfully resolved!

Thank You, Thank You, Thank You. It is people like you that truly make a difference in this world. Your dedication to serving the needs of agents like myself is what makes representing a company like National Life so important to me. Your willingness to go above and beyond to assist me should not go without noting. Please forward my message to your boss and your boss's boss on my behalf.

Your patience and compassionate spirit has truly left me believing that there are still wonderful people like yourself in this world who are willing to help others.

We would like to pass along a well-deserved note of appreciation to Nicole on the new business desk. She is consistently very positive and professional. She is a great representative for National Life. If there is a company award or recognition for excellent service, I would like to nominate her.

TO MANY, THE PEOPLE OF NATIONAL LIFE ARE BETTER KNOWN AS THE "DO GOODERS."

These Do Gooders are also developing long-term, trusted relationships with the agents they sell through. Agents know National Life and National Life knows their agents. In 2014, National Life increased its distribution channel by 37 percent and grew life insurance sales by 30 percent when the rest of the industry's life sales were flat. Distribution is growing as National Life's story spreads throughout the industry.

In early 2015, after leading a town hall forum at National Life, Mehran was stopped by a colleague who said, "Boy, you sound like you are on a crusade."

Mehran pleaded guilty. He is on a crusade. As he travels the country meeting with agents, prospective employees, and colleagues, he carries the message that the industry is special. Mehran believes they're doing heroic work and the profession is about love.

As sentimental as it may sound, there is truth to it. The insurance industry takes care of families and takes care of businesses by ensuring that families stay together and businesses and legacies continue. Mehran passionately believes the industry offers a safety net for life, retirement, AND death. National Life products are more than just death benefits. Their products are beneficial if you die too soon, live too long, or suffer an illness.

According to a not-for-profit insurance advocacy group, LifeHappens.org "You buy life insurance because you love someone." They affectionately refer to life insurance as love insurance. On their website they post a series of real life stories featuring dramatic accounts of families and businesses whose financial well-being was safeguarded by the benefits of insurance and the work of insurance professionals. Use the QR code on page 36 to watch "Life Happens."

"LIFE HAPPENS—LOVE INSURANCE: A LEGACY OF LOVE."

Life happens and life unscripted happens too. Unfortunately, when it does it can set off an avalanche of disruptions.

> *We keep alive the dreams of families, the hopes of small business owners, and the dignity and financial independence of seniors. In my view, no profession can be more honorable or special.*
>
> Mehran Assadi

MOTIVATED BY A MORAL IMPERATIVE

If you've been in the insurance industry or any industry for a while, you understand the power of using meetings to keep people informed and motivated. Inspiring music, pep talks from six-figure colleagues who have built extremely successful careers, new product roll outs from the corporate folks, and a lot of stomping, cheering, and high-fiving.

It's all good. Coaching and mentoring relationships are established, networks expand, friendships grow deeper, and "newbies" catch the adrenaline rush of what's possible. Who's not for that?

THE PROBLEM IS THE RUSH DOESN'T LAST.

The rush is temporary at best, which is why National Life keeps having these meetings, right? We are NOT, for even a minute, suggesting people should stop having meetings. The atmosphere of lifelong learning and personal growth at these events is critical. And we wholeheartedly believe you are known by the company you keep. Rubbing shoulders with and learning from people who will never be satisfied with life or business-as-usual is a good thing. These kinds of events draw the best out of people. And who doesn't want to be part of an incredible community of like-minded people who want to enrich lives?

But to produce something that lasts, something that inspires a deep-seated, long-term contribution to the business and the movement, requires more than a shot of adrenaline every 90 days.

WHAT'S NEEDED IS A MORAL IMPERATIVE.

BEHIND ALL GREAT ORGANIZATIONS IS A SENSE OF DUTY THAT INSPIRES PEOPLE TO ACT IN CERTAIN WAYS.

At ING Direct, founding CEO Arkadi Kuhlmann set out to champion customers who were being preyed on by the traditional banking industry. Although ING has been acquired by Capital One, the original mission was to achieve a moral imperative: to lead people back to saving by simplifying financial products without charging extortionist fees.

Apple is driven by a desire to enrich people's lives with a whole ecosystem of elegant products that are ultra-user-friendly.

DEMOCRATIZING ASSURANCE! A VERY CLEAR MORAL IMPERATIVE.

At Medtronic, the moral imperative is alleviating pain; at Humana, it's creating lifelong well-being for everyone; for Google, it's organizing the world's information and making it universally accessible and useful.

MORAL IMPERATIVE = SENSE OF PURPOSE AND DESTINY.

A moral imperative is visceral. It doesn't come from advertising spin, sophisticated advisors, or slick sales agents. And it's certainly not something you gin up just to wring more out of people so they will make their numbers. It doesn't live on the wall or on a glossy card; it lives in people's hearts.

THIS IS WHAT MAKES IT SO COMPELLING.

Out of 938 life insurance providers in the U.S., National Life is moving from relevance to prominence. It is recognized as #19 of the top 20 providers in the country as measured in life sales.

AT A TIME WHEN INDUSTRY LIFE SALES ARE FLAT, NATIONAL LIFE SALES ARE INCREASING TO RECORD LEVELS.

America is a melting pot and National Life holds a special ingredient that has the power to help the unique communities within this diverse nation realize the American Dream.

DEMOCRATIZING ASSURANCE—MAKING IT AVAILABLE TO EVERYONE IS A VERY CLEAR MORAL IMPERATIVE.

When life unscripted throws you a curve, protection, peace of mind, and life assurance matter. National Life is filled with people who share their passion, voice, talent, friendship, and benefits for life because they are motivated by and committed to this moral imperative.

In observing the people of National Life we fully understand that you don't have to join AmeriCorps to serve. We have seen time and time again that you can join a company like National Life and serve.

No company and no nation can outperform its aspirations.

The heights to which we rise depend on the weightiness of our dreams.

National Life works for TRANSFORMATIONAL as opposed to incremental change.

Our LIVES begin to end the day we become SILENT about things that MATTER.

Martin Luther King, Jr.

Indra Nooyi,
Chairman & CEO, PepsiCo

PART 3
IN GOOD COMPANY
PURPOSE DRIVEN AND CAUSE ORIENTED

NOT JUST SUGAR WATER

N ational Life is in good company. Even huge multinational firms are reinventing WHY and HOW they do business. Yet National Life still occupies that rarified space among companies that have been cause-oriented for over 100 years.

Seven years ago, Indra Nooyi, Chairman and CEO of PepsiCo, launched a far-reaching program that would, in many ways, redefine the way PepsiCo does business. She called it:

PERFORMANCE WITH PURPOSE.

Nooyi sees PepsiCo's success as inextricably linked to the success of the world in which it operates. And for PepsiCo the geography gets really big really fast. Pepsi's products are used by consumers a billion times a day in over 200 countries.

Performance with a Purpose has four major focus areas: Performance, Human Sustainability, Environmental Sustainability, and Talent Sustainability. PepsiCo believes these goals will position the company for long-term, sustainable growth by aligning what is good for its business with what is good for society and the planet. According to Nooyi,

Performance with Purpose is not a defined set of issues, a collection of goals or metrics, or something of interest only to a select set of stakeholders. It is quite simply the way all of us at PepsiCo do business...It is delivering results in the right way, in a sustained way. It means we live our values and do so in a way that fuels our performance. We like to think of it as the way we strive to "future-proof" PepsiCo.

With a company that spans the globe many times over, it's mind-boggling just how pervasive this cause is. Here are just a few examples of what PepsiCo is doing that show the company is walking the talk.

Inspired by Performance with Purpose, Food for Good is a social enterprise within the company that utilizes PepsiCo's logistics, delivery vehicles, warehouse facilities, and management skills to make nutrition accessible for low-income families in the U.S. Since 2009 this initiative has served more than 2.5 million meals to those in need. And it doesn't stop there. In partnership with another organization, Feeding America, PepsiCo volunteers packaged an estimated 705,000 meals for hungry families.

The World Economic Forum has identified water supply crises as among the world's top five risks. Approximately 70 percent of our water supply is consumed in agriculture. And, it is often the food and beverage industry's most-used resource. PepsiCo won the Stockholm Industry Water Award in 2012 and the U.S. Water Prize in 2013, among other awards, for its water efficiency programs which achieved more than 14 billion liters in water flow savings.

Another initiative funded by PepsiCo in Asia-Pacific is WaterHope, a social enterprise that builds water stations to provide safe, clean, and affordable water to thousands of people in disadvantaged communities.

Each WaterHope station includes a community center that houses dental, medical, and legal clinics, as well as daycare centers for young children who might otherwise be left home alone while their parents work. The impact is significant. For example, in the last six years WaterHope Philippines provided clean drinking water to more than 1.5 million people.

Economic empowerment for women by training them to become entrepreneurs. Literacy skills and self-esteem for girls. It's all part of the company's effort to endorse and embrace the United Nation's Women's Empowerment Principles—Equity Means Business. These principles guide companies like PepsiCo with regard to how they empower women in the workplace, marketplace, and community.

NOT AT TANDUS, S
A CHANGE AG

N ORDINARY WORK

Recognizing what the research has now supported for years—that teams are stronger whenever women are present—PepsiCo is also aggressively working to increase the number of female executives and women leaders within the company.

PepsiCo's cause, Performance with Purpose, is not tangential; it's a powerful rallying cry that has united and motivated the people of PepsiCo to make a difference all over the world. While Indra Nooyi believes that the company still has so much to accomplish, this cause has been, and will continue to be, the catalyst in the transformation of one of the world's most famous brands.

Where do the financial and sustainability issues begin and end? What distinguishes sustainability performance from financial performance? Do you invest and reinvest more in sustainability performance or financial performance? Indra Nooyi would tell you, "They are one and the same."

NOT JUST CARPET

Tandus Centiva, a Tarkett Company, is not just a global flooring company—they are the global leader in closed-loop recycling. With a history dating to 1803, Tandus Centiva has built a legacy on quality, performance, design, and social responsibility. In 1994, they launched the first closed-loop recycling program in the carpet industry.

TALENT SUSTAINABILITY

Mary Head, Plant Manager, and her manufacturing co-workers were looking for a way to recycle used carpet. They thought, "WHAT IF we could repurpose that prehistoric extruder that's collecting dust on the factory floor?" So Mary called the manufacturer of the machine for some engineering advice. The experts said, "Interesting idea, BUT it can't be done—it won't work."

Mary disagreed and chose to find a way to repurpose the extruder and use it to recycle old carpet and waste materials. Mary was ambitious; she took on what the experts said was impossible! She began teaching herself how to reconfigure various components to control feeding, pressure, heat, and extrusion. The result? A socially responsible innovation.

Mary and her team created the very first carpet-recycling machine. This led to a process now known as closed-loop recycling. To date, more than 268 million pounds of carpet, LVT (luxury vinyl tile), and waste have been recycled, repurposed, and reused. This means that not another square inch of used carpet ever has to go into a landfill. Mary's choice to own and run with an idea continues to have a powerful positive impact on the environment.

90,000
LBS

ENVIRONMENTAL SUSTAINABILITY

Mary challenged the industry and inspired change; she chose to be a change maker, serve her team, innovate for the company, and engage in contagious environmental stewardship. She ignited a movement of other people within Tandus Centiva who are also committed to sustainability, innovation, and responsibility— people who have an unending quest to make a positive and lasting impact in the world. The company now monitors five keys to environmental sustainability: water, energy, waste, recycling, and emissions.

Today, their Dalton, Georgia, environmental center is the industry's first and only third-party certified reclamation facility that uses the closed-loop system. The reclamation program enables them to include all post-consumer take-back carpet and pre-consumer carpet waste into new recycled floor coverings. Waste to landfill is now less than 0.1 ounce per square yard of manufactured goods.

In addition, their **closed-loop recycling process** has enabled the company to almost completely eliminate all manufacturing carpet and LVT waste. Currently, their waste to landfill is less than 1 percent by weight of its total manufacturing production, and they are fully committed to achieving continuous percentage decreases.

Tandus Centiva has **reduced its water usage** by leveraging closed-loop systems to recycle process water. They are committed to purchasing capital equipment with water-saving features and eliminating certain wet processes. Tandus Centiva's Florence, Alabama LVT plant has achieved 0 percent production waste water.

They also require annual **greenhouse gas inventories** for all of their facilities as well as showrooms and offices. They have reduced their global greenhouse gas emissions by 15 percent per square yard, since their baseline year in 2006. And where available, facilities have participated in the Green Power Switch program offered by local utility providers.

Tandus Centiva employs a multi-faceted approach to **reducing the carbon footprint** of its operations and its products, including the reduction of energy, water, and solid waste; the increased use of renewable energy and biofuel; and, of course, Tandus Centiva's continued commitment to closed-loop recycling and post-consumer reclamation of its products.

We need more companies that inspire people everywhere to challenge the status quo and to look beyond business-as-usual by asking, "What if?" **Tandus Centiva is doing good one carpet at a time.**

NOT JUST RETAIL

Like PepsiCo, Lululemon also believes it has a role to play in helping to address some of the world's most pressing health challenges, including obesity and other lifestyle-related challenges. Founded in 1998 by Chip Wilson, Lululemon Athletica is a yoga-inspired athletic apparel company that forgoes following fashion cycles or trends and chooses to embody a lifestyle above all else. The Lululemon lifestyle spans international and online borders and offers both women and men a holistic perspective on health and well-being.

HUMAN SUSTAINABILITY

Unlike most retailers, Lululemon's teams of die-hard brand ambassadors, known internally as in-store educators, are passionate about disrupting the retail experience (its stores sell nearly $2,000/sq. ft.) by bringing its vision/cause to life: **"elevating the world from mediocrity to greatness."** How? At Lululemon you are more than a job description and when you join their team, "it's not a job, it's a journey." As a matter of fact, Lululemon believes in a lot of lofty things:

> *Sweat once a day. Live within your means but above your expectations. Floss. Above all, we believe in self-empowerment, positive inner-development and taking responsibility for our own lives. A Lululemon career is more than what you do today. It's what you're going to do tomorrow.*

It is not unusual for team members to say, "I'm a completely different person for having worked for Lululemon."

Their stores are designed to be the heart and soul of the brand, places that inspire greatness. Employee growth is encouraged from day one. All employees are asked and expected to share short- and long-term career, health, and personal goals, as well as habits and routines that get in their way. Team members are also expected to hold each other accountable to achieving their goals and living the Lululemon mantra by sharing feedback from a place of kindness. Employees can attend their choice of local fitness classes and events—races, spin, CrossFit, yoga—all paid for by the company. Not only is it a perk to have healthy behavior paid for; it also allows employees to create authentic relationships with potential customers and like-minded community ambassadors. By working out with the locals in the community, employees can spread the word about Lululemon organically. In addition, they can connect and recruit other fitness-minded people to become "ambassadors" who can then receive special discounts in exchange for representing the brand in the community.

In the spirit of inspiring healthy communities for employees and customers alike, Lululemon educators and team leaders strive to make each store a hub of conversation, connection, engagement, and overall well-being (fit body and mind). For example, most retailers sell a brand this way: "Come into our stores, and when you buy, wear, and use our stuff then you can 'Be Cool' too." At Lululemon, they sell the brand with a humanizing twist; the brand says, **"You're already cool, we just want to be your partner in bringing out your best possible self."**

In-store community boards provide connections to yoga classes, running clubs, goal setting workshops, and aspirational postings. Store educators are encouraged to bring Lululemon's famous red bag mantra to life by "making someone's day better, suggesting a new workout, inspiring someone to achieve a personal goal, or simply offering support."

The Lululemon mantra and company vision have become powerful recruiting tools as well; they draw in those who self-identify with the Lululemon lifestyle. In fact, most employees were customers first. Employees live and breathe the mantra, which creates a rare experience on the retail floor because employees are proud to work there. The vision and lifestyle mantra also serves to motivate employees to give themselves more fully to their work; they opt-in because the company values are in keeping with their own values. So, instead of feeling like their job is to push stuff onto unsuspecting customers, Lululemon educators  are encouraged to form relationships and grow a community of brand advocates. Sounds much more meaningful, doesn't it?

The Lululemon approach to transcending mediocrity translates into positive customer experiences and a better bottom line. The company numbers continue to prove the critics on Wall Street wrong. Revenue is climbing, its stock is up, and sales are on the rise, in all categories, in store and online.

FAR-REACHING SUSTAINABILITY

Today more than ever we need people who face challenges, see opportunities, and want to effect change. At Lululemon the vision is big. It involves more than elevating people; the vision is to elevate the world from mediocrity to greatness by embracing social, environmental, and economic health in every part of the organization and

in all their global communities. Their BHAG (Big Hairy Audacious Goal) is to completely blur the lines between what are considered social, environmental, and economic initiatives by celebrating solutions that speak to all three. How?

In addition to what goes on in-store, they too are taking steps to reduce their environmental footprint across all areas of the business. But, for Lululemon sustainability is about more than working to reduce an organization's impact on the environment. They work with global partners that share their values and they give without expectation. In yoga, mettā is the practice of generating love and happiness for others. It is deeply rooted in the belief of giving without expectation, and is a critical step on the path to personal growth. Through their Mettā Movement—a grassroots community philanthropy program—Lululemon provides funds to stores, area managers, employees, suppliers, and ambassadors to launch and support projects like Room to Read in Cambodia, 30 days of OM in California, Surf Rider Clean up in Florida, Edible Garden in Vancouver, and the Africa Yoga Project in Kenya, all projects that contribute to social and environmental health.

With global obesity and other health and wellness concerns on the rise and employee engagement and human connection on the decline, Lululemon's approach to disrupting the retail experience offers a holistic approach to improving lives. We need more **change makers, educators, brand ambassadors, and global partners who are doing good business by inspiring customers to rise above mediocrity and strive for greatness.**

The big point here is that National Life is and has been on the forefront of really cool companies, companies that define themselves in terms of a cause. But again, what attracted us to National Life is that they were cause-oriented before cause was cool.

National Life prides itself on offering employees opportunities to "Experience Life." On campus the company has a par course; snow shoe, hiking and running trails; and bicycles outside the company gym for employees to use when they need a break.

Recently, one employee shared that he left his previous company in Boston, Massachusetts, because he'd rather get stuck in a line for the chair lift at a local ski resort than in city traffic.

Every month, employees on both campuses in Vermont and Texas are encouraged to step away from their desks and take a 20-minute walk with a walking group. In addition, all employees are encouraged and paid to take 40 hours a year to participate in volunteer projects.

Like other mission-driven companies, by doing good for employees National Life is creating brand ambassadors. When employees and agents have positive experiences at work, a movement starts and this movement helps with recruiting, reputation, and sales.

But these days doing good for employees isn't just about cool perks, it's also about creating a collaborative work environment where people can build stronger relationships, not just to experience life, but to experience each other as well. This requires a fresh approach to leadership and collaboration. Leadership today doesn't mean the leader has all the answers, but rather, the leader is gifted at getting others to think about being social architects of the culture and work environment in order to gain great ideas from everyone. That means fostering the freedom to share ideas, reach across functional boundaries, collaborate, and innovate.

Cool companies are finding creative approaches to re-imagine corporate space, hierarchies, functional boundaries, silos/tribes, and even traditional roles to re-create a place where everyone individually can share ideas to achieve collective innovation, change, and improvement.

Mehran recently tore down sky-high office cubicles and transformed the work environment at National Life to a more open workplace with glass conference rooms. And in an effort to be in the middle of the action and break traditional hierarchies, he moved from the first floor Executive Offices to an open office on their fifth floor, a floor he considers to be the lifeblood of the company, marketing and distribution.

Not too long after his move Mehran interviewed a candidate for an Associate General Agent position in his newly acquired fish bowl, all glass, open office. The candidate, who was also being courted by four other insurance companies, was not only impressed with the fact that Mehran was the only CEO he had an interview with, but he also couldn't wait to call his wife and tell her that National Life is more like Google than any other company he'd visited.

Now let's go deeper and discover what's behind this piqued interest in purpose-driven companies and how cause inspires passion, drives culture, and can fuel a movement.

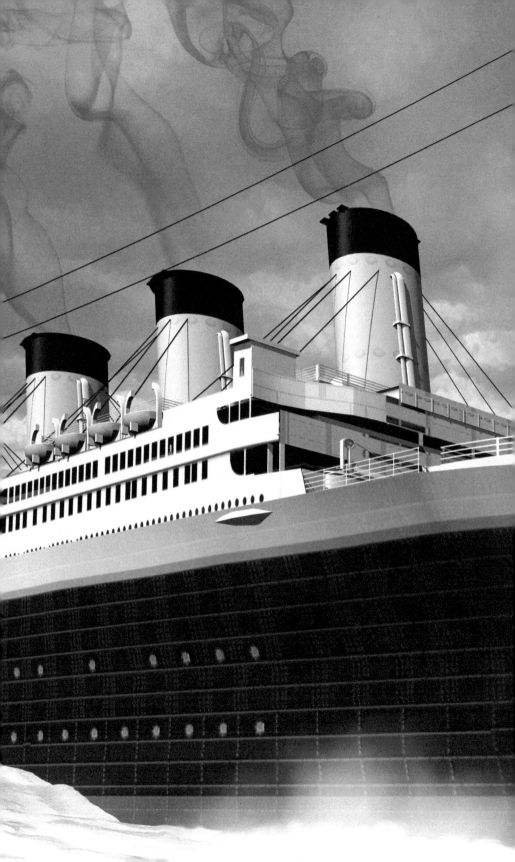

PART 4
WHAT REALLY MOTIVATES YOU?

THE FILMS WE LOVE ARE TELLING US SOMETHING—WE LONG TO BE PART OF
SOMETHING EPIC!

- Titanic
- Top Gun
- Rob Roy
- Gladiator
- Star Wars
- The Matrix
- The Lord of the Rings
- The Patriot
- Braveheart
- The Hobbit
- Joan of Arc
- Robin Hood
- Schindler's List

WHAT WILL MOVE YOU TO BRING IT!

THE GREATEST NEEDS OF HUMAN EXISTENCE

WORK THAT MATTERS.

WORK THAT IS MEANINGFUL.

WORK THAT MAKES A DIFFERENCE.

Isn't that what we all want? Isn't that what every company needs if its most talented people are to become fully engaged?

Lifting society up, creating a better world, serving others—that's what it means to be fully human.

Deny this and you run the risk of dehumanizing the very people who are essential to your success. It's like asking them to bring only a part of themselves to work every day.

Interested in learning what ultimately drives us?

If you could build a business that taps into our greatest needs, how would you do it?

Want to know where motivation, commitment, and dedication come from?

Read on...

WIRED FOR HEROISM

PEOPLE AREN'T AFRAID OF DYING—THEY'RE AFRAID OF NOT HAVING LIVED.

Planted in every one of us is a seed. It's called DESIRE. We have a deep-seated desire to do something heroic with our lives. Not heroic in the sense of celebrity, fame, or fortune, but rather heroic as in doing something with our lives that is eternally important.

Some of us are clearly in touch with it; others sometimes sense that it's there, but years of resignation have made it difficult to see and hard to access.

We long for more and know we were made for more, but "more" has eluded us so many times that we've told ourselves: It's better to compromise your heart, lower your expectations, and bury your desire than risk the prospect of being disappointed. This is as good as it gets. Live with it.

BUT THE LONGING FOR MEANING AND SIGNIFICANCE REFUSES TO BE THWARTED. IT HAS BEEN HARDWIRED INTO US.

In 1972 Ernest Becker won a Pulitzer Prize for writing ***The Denial of Death.*** Becker said that what people fear most in life is not dying, it's dying with a sense of insignificance. It's the frightening, unsettling feeling you get when you see death, lurking over the horizon, marching its way to your doorstep, and you ask:

DID MY LIFE COUNT FOR ANYTHING? DID I MAKE A MARK IN THE WORLD?

DID I DO ANYTHING THAT WAS TRULY MEANINGFUL?

Scary questions. They force us to look at our lives. The people who have the most difficult time with dying are those who feel they haven't done anything worthwhile in their lives. How many people have you met who, when confronted with terminal illness, pray for just a few more years to get it right?

Heroism is about engaging in work that ultimately enriches peoples' lives and makes the world a better place. It's about creating a legacy you won't regret or want to apologize for.

THE PHILOSOPHER HORACE KALLEN MARKED HIS 73RD BIRTHDAY BY WRITING:

There are persons who shape their lives by the fear of death, and persons who shape their lives by the joy and satisfaction of life. The former live dying; the latter die living. I know that fate may stop me tomorrow, but death is an irrelevant contingency. Whenever it comes, I intend to die living.

ISN'T THAT THE DESIRE IN EACH OF US—THAT WE SHALL DIE LIVING, ALL USED UP SERVING A PURPOSE OR CAUSE GREATER THAN OURSELVES?

GREAT COMPANIES
HELP PEOPLE FIND THE HEROISM IN THEIR WORK

Heroic work is adventurous. It tests our character and our talents as we stretch to pursue extraordinary things.

To be part of an organization where you truly believe that your work is heroic is a WOW. It is a source of fulfillment, satisfaction, and joy. It enables you to plug into a source of energy and enthusiasm you didn't even know you had. Heroic work raises your esteem for what you do and unleashes something in you that says, "I want to do it even better."

SO, WHAT'S THE PROBLEM?

People are wired for heroism, yet our incentive systems and compensation plans are generally geared toward MONEY and THINGS. Nothing's wrong with this except that the adrenaline rush from money and things quickly wanes. The buzz wears off quicker than we think it will. Then, we wonder why we burn out trying to bring more people in the front door because we are hemorrhaging people out the back door who are no longer inspired.

We justify it by saying, "It's a numbers game." That is, you have to recruit a lot of people to find the truly great ones who are serious about and capable of building a business. When we lose people, we rationalize it by saying, "They just weren't meant for this type of business." We completely overlook the fact that our people are made to do something heroic with their lives.

You will never motivate the best people with money alone. Yes, money matters. You can't pay the bills without money and a business must be profitable to survive. Cash flow enables us to do a lot of important things. It just doesn't inspire long-term engagement and greatness.

Study the job satisfaction surveys. Money is never at the top of the list of things that motivate people at work. People want to be engaged in work that matters. Work that expresses our truest gifts and addresses our deepest needs while creating a better world is heroic.

GO BACK
TO WORK.
CHANGE
THE WORLD.

WHAT IF WE GAVE PEOPLE A COMPELLING REASON TO STAY?

What if the business was defined as a cause that gives people the opportunity to do something noble, something that inspires them to shout,

"I'M ALL IN!"

When you do this genuinely and consistently, people will beat a path to your door.

WHAT DRIVES GREATNESS?

An opportunity to give HISTORY A SHOVE,

An invitation to CHANGE THE WORLD, and

A deep-seated belief that it is actually POSSIBLE!

For too long we have been dreaming a dream from which we are now waking up: the dream that if we just improve the socio-economic situation of people, everything will be okay, people will become happy. The truth is that as the struggle for survival subsides, the question emerges: Survival for what? Ever more people today have the means to live, but no meaning to live for.

Viktor Frankl
Man's Search for Meaning

THE SEARCH FOR MEANING

WHY DO WE HAVE SUCH A NEED TO MAKE OUR LIVES COUNT?

WHERE DOES OUR STRUGGLE WITH INSIGNIFICANCE COME FROM?

First, what steals joy in our lives is the absence of meaning. We just don't do well when we feel that our lives are arbitrary, random, and pointless. If you conclude that you have no meaning in life, you will start to feel hopeless which leaves room for boredom and discontent, fear and anxiety, cynicism and bitterness, or depression and despair to grow.

OUR SOULS CRAVE A REASON TO LIVE.

In ***Man's Search for Meaning*** (12 million copies sold), Viktor Frankl describes life inside the Nazi concentration camps during World War II. Frankl lived in three different death camps including Auschwitz. While he survived, his mother, father, and wife did not.

Frankl said that those who survived the horrors of the death camps were not necessarily the strong, healthy, or able-bodied; it was those who had a sense of hope fueled by something important they had left to do in life. These survivors had something yet to live for which gave their lives meaning and gave them hope.

Meaning isn't something we just get when we go on a journey to "find ourselves." Meaning is created and discovered when we become deeply committed to someone or something we truly believe in. That's why those (even those with considerable wealth) who have no commitments often struggle to find meaning in their lives.

This is the true joy in life, the being
used for a purpose recognized by
yourself as a mighty one; the being
thoroughly worn out before you are
thrown on the scrap heap; the being a
force of Nature instead of a feverish
selfish little clod of ailments and
grievances complaining that the
world will not devote itself to
making you happy.

George Bernard Shaw
Man and Superman

NO MEANING, NO HAPPINESS

HAPPINESS.

Isn't that what we all want? Ask any parent what they want for their children. The response will be some version of: I just want them to be happy.

WE'VE GOT NEWS FOR YOU.

You don't become happy by pursuing happiness. You become happy by living a life that matters, a life filled with meaning and significance. And that comes from being committed to something beyond yourself.

If you don't have a sense of purpose, a cause worth fighting for, it's much easier to become self-absorbed and preoccupied with your own desire for happiness. The more obsessed with it you are, the more it eludes you. Because whatever you think will make you happy is never enough. There's always someone richer, smarter, more skilled, better looking, or happier than you. People who pursue happiness, in and of itself, usually end up unhappy, longing for more.

WHO DO YOU THINK ARE THE HAPPIEST PEOPLE AROUND?

Are they the current pop culture icons? The famous CEOs? The superstar athletes? Those who seem to have it all? We doubt it. Are they the self-enlightenment folks who move from one self-help fad to the next but never get grounded or comfortable in their own skin? Nope.

We suspect the happiest people are the ones who "live loved" because they know they are loved. And they know this because of the commitment, self-sacrifice, kindness, generosity, and grace extended to them by others. We're betting the happiest people you know are the ones who are caught up in a cause that has something to do with enriching the human condition.

You'll never find happiness by looking for it. You will find it, serendipitously, through serving, loving, and fighting for something that lightens the load of others. George Bernard Shaw makes this point precisely in *Man and Superman*.

THE WORLD ISN'T HERE TO MAKE US HAPPY.

We were given our gifts and talents to serve the world. And when we figure out how to do this in the context of being committed to something noble and heroic—something that makes the world better—joy, fulfillment, and, yes, sometimes even happiness are the natural byproducts that sneak in the backdoor and land upon our souls.

> I don't know what your destiny will be, but one thing I know: the only ones among you who will be really happy are those who have sought and found how to serve.
>
> Albert Schweitzer
> Nobel Peace Prize, 1952

BRING LIFE
TO
WHAT WE DO

A LIFE THAT MATTERS

Most of us can accept that the stories of our lives have a beginning, middle, and end. But what we ultimately want to know is:

WAS THE STORY WORTH READING?

Our dear friends lost their 14-year-old daughter to heart disease. Time ran out as she was waiting for a heart transplant. In the wake of her death her mom has dedicated much of her life to promoting organ donation. It is unbearable for any of us to think that this young child died in vain. So our friend is doing what she can to ensure that her daughter's short life wasn't wasted. Her passion to make something good come out of this terrible tragedy is, in one sense, an act of rebellion. It's her expression of an intolerable "No!" to a life of insignificance. The cause she fights for is her way of giving her daughter's life meaning, of making sure that because her daughter lived, the world is a better place.

How many of us have been to an older friend's funeral and heard the eulogy describe the person as a dirty, rotten scoundrel, a lousy spouse, or an inept businessperson? It never happens. Because something deep inside of us can't tolerate the idea that a person lived and it didn't matter. So, we dig deep to find the accolades.

THE LONGING OF OUR SOULS, LIVING A LIFE THAT MATTERS.

The human need for significance is immeasurable. Everyone wants to know that they are important, that they matter, and that the world takes them seriously. Yet, how can we build lives that matter if we aren't engaged in work that matters?

A life that matters is what drives scientists and researchers to find a cure for disease. It's what drives medical pioneers like the late Dr. Michael DeBakey to invent one medical breakthrough after another. It's what drives rock stars like Bono of U2 to leverage his celebrity to eliminate extreme poverty in Africa. It's what drives entrepreneurs like Herb Kelleher at Southwest Airlines to democratize the skies or Ratan Tata to give people in rural India a $2,500 car so they can safely drive to the cities where there is job opportunity, healthcare, and education.

And the same is true for Mehran Assadi, President and CEO of National Life, a man who loves insurance and a man on a crusade to move National Life from relevance to prominence. How? By serving the most underserved demographic in this country, Middle America. Assadi is on a mission to democratize financial literacy, protection, entrepreneurship and promises that allow you to capitalize on

FOR THE SECRET OF MAN'S BEING IS NOT ONLY TO LIVE, BUT TO HAVE SOMETHING TO LIVE FOR.

Fyodor Dostoyevsky

the assurance of living a life of dignity without having to die first. National Life has turned the stereotype that all financial services companies are greedy and cold into one that genuinely cares for its customers, its employees, its agents and the communities in which it's based.

THESE ENTREPRENEURS ARE ACTIVISTS. THEY MAKE WORK A CAUSE.

Their ingenuity is the result of a deep-seated need to solve a problem that could change history. Unpack their motives and you will find the same intolerable "No!" expressed by our friends who lost their daughter. It's as if they are saying,

"No, I will not just get by. No, I will not waste the gifts and talents I've been given. No, I will not play small. I will not walk past this problem. I will leave the world a better place for having passed through it."

"I WILL LIVE A LIFE THAT MATTERS."

DID TODAY REALLY MATTER?

HERE TO BELONG

If being loved and accepted are among the greatest needs of human existence, then rejection, alienation, isolation, loneliness, and anonymity are among our greatest fears. If you doubt this, ask yourself, "Why do we use solitary confinement as a form of punishment? Why do our greatest joys and deepest wounds have to do with relationships?"

WE WANT TO BELONG.

We are relational to the core. The literature is loaded with evidence suggesting that caring, affectionate bonds from close relationships are a major key to wellness. People who feel part of a community generally have a higher level of happiness and well-being than those who don't.

Now, when that community endeavors to tackle a big, hairy problem that matters, people bond more quickly. And with each enemy the community faces, relationships grow stronger because an outside foe often draws people into relationships that have greater emotional depth.

UNFORTUNATELY, TODAY MORE AND MORE OF US FEEL DISCOUNTED.

Take a flight to almost anywhere, call your mobile carrier, check on your insurance claim, or try to reconcile a statement with your bank. What do you discover? You're invisible. You don't matter. In a world that treats us so indifferently, we feel objectified, dehumanized, and anonymous. It's hard to take responsibility for creating a better world when you feel disconnected, anonymous, and powerless.

WHY DO WE JOIN THE MILITARY, ASSOCIATIONS, TEAMS, CLUBS, AND FAITH-BASED COMMUNITIES?

They provide us with a sense of identity and a place to share common aspirations. They create an opportunity for us to connect, be heard, and be supported. When we feel heard, we also feel validated. And, collectively, we have more power to effect change, to make a difference.

We join movements and fight for causes because we see ourselves locking arms with others, playing an important role in a bigger story—an epic story.

AND WE BELONG.

VISION & MISSION

OXYGEN FOR THE SOUL

If you want to make a difference in people's lives and build a business that draws the very best out of others, you must get this.

THE YEARNING FOR HEROISM,

THE SEARCH FOR MEANING,

THE DESIRE TO LIVE A LIFE THAT MATTERS, AND

THE NEED TO BELONG ARE AMONG THE GREATEST NEEDS OF HUMAN EXISTENCE.

During a visit to the Vermont campus we ran into Chris Graff, National Life Vice President of Communications, who spoke to this very need when he described the role Mehran has played in transforming the culture of National Life:

> *Mehran refocused us on our mission; he also crafted a vision statement and set of values that were easy for all to remember and live by. Our future is clear. We are building upon our rich history as a legacy to continue. Today we are focused and committed to fulfilling the vision that National Life is a "national" company that serves a critical purpose. We are proud of what we do. We are excited by what we do.*

You will never understand what ultimately drives you and what ultimately motivates the people you lead until you understand this:

We are most ALIVE and engaged when we have a sense of destiny, when we feel called to something greater than ourselves. And, when we give ourselves to that calling, it changes us and makes us better; we become stronger and more capable of doing extraordinary things.

We were born with the imagination to create, the will to achieve, the capacity to accomplish, the heart to serve, and, most importantly, the desire to love and be loved.

GREAT COMPANIES START
BECAUSE THE FOUNDERS WANT TO
CHANGE THE WORLD
NOT MAKE A FAST BUCK

It's not as if we push an "off" button when we walk through the front door at work and these needs cease to exist. If we can't satisfy these longings at work, out of frustration we slowly and consistently begin to "tolerate" work and seek fulfillment somewhere else.

Author Daniel Pink observed that although we have staggering levels of disengagement at work, there is a significant rise in volunteerism. Apparently, volunteerism is nourishing our deepest needs in ways that the work we get paid for isn't.

OUR SOULS LONG FOR MORE AT WORK.

What if we could create a culture at work that "juiced" us in the same way volunteerism does?

What if we could create a business that offers the kind of inspiration for the soul that we get when pursuing a cause that has won our hearts, minds, and spirits?

WE CAN AND WE SHOULD, BECAUSE THERE'S A PROBLEM.

DEAD PEOPLE WORKIN

PART 5
WAKING THE DEAD
WARNING!

MAJOR EPIDEMIC THREATENS BUSINESS.

T hink about the people you know in business. How many are totally fired up and impassioned about what they do? How many are bored and frustrated? How many people do you know who would say, if they were honest, that they dread Mondays?

There's an epidemic sweeping businesses today—from the largest Fortune 500 firms to the little mom-and-pop deli on Main Street. This epidemic threatens not only the success and prosperity of businesses themselves but also nothing less than the long-term economic standing of every nation in the world. The epidemic?

DEAD PEOPLE WORKING!

You know them because many of you work with them. They are in the next cubicle, down the hall, in your department, in the call center, and, yes, even on the executive team. They are physically present, but they are psychologically, emotionally, and intellectually checked out.

Many of these people do the worst thing possible. To use a phrase coined by our friend Ken Blanchard, they…

QUIT, BUT STAY.

Some stay busy and pretend that all is well while dying a little bit inside each day. Some live for weekends, holidays, and for the things outside of work that bring meaning to their lives. Some become toxic complainers deriving some sick sense of significance from stirring things up at work.

MOST OF THEM COME TO WORK ON MONDAY MORNING DOA (DEAD ON ARRIVAL).

We continue to be stunned by the level of resignation, victimization, emptiness, and ultimately deadness that so many people have learned to live with in the workplace. Gallup reports that 51 percent of the global workforce is not engaged at work and 18 percent is actively disengaged. That's 69 percent of the workforce that isn't firing on all cylinders! And, unfortunately, these statistics haven't changed much in ten years.

You cannot compete in the world today without innovation and you can't innovate without a steady flow of fresh ideas from people who are turned on, engaged, and fired up about what they are doing.

If only one in eight people we know are fully engaged in and enthusiastic about their jobs, our businesses are in serious trouble.

This is costing our organizations billions. It stunts the economic growth of these businesses and diminishes the quality of life for the people who work in them.

WE CAN DO BETTER.

The most successful organizations never stand still They are always looking for ways to do things better; they are always seeking to reinvent themselves, aiming even higher.

Mehran Assadi

From everything we've seen National Life isn't just better, they are among the BEST! They are one of the top twenty insurance providers in the United States. National Life ranks among many of the most highly rated according to A.M. Best, Standard and Poor's, and Moody's. And they remain an employer of choice in all of their local markets.

Every other Monday during new hire orientation the new hires are asked why they chose to come to work for National Life. Nine out of 10 respond that "it's the culture, they want to make a difference and contribute to the cause."

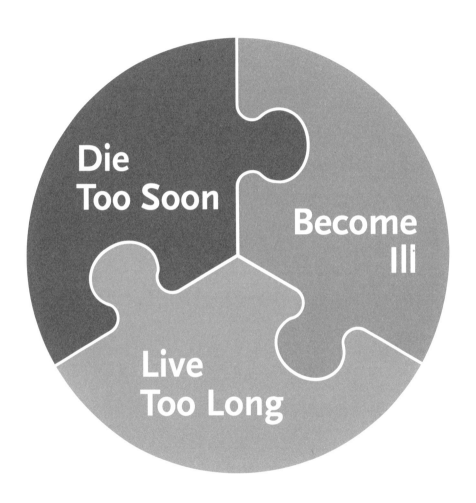

Die
Too Soon

Become
Ill

Live
Too Long

Recently a team of National Life IT and business associates didn't just look for a way to make something better, they successfully implemented a better system. A business processing model, known internally as the Technology and Operations Platform (TOPP) Project, was launched in 2014 in an effort to transform how National Life and most other insurance companies conduct business. It was designed and built to host their first proprietary life product as a truly end-to-end process. For ten months teams in both the Montpelier and Dallas offices collaborated to build an industry "first" that will allow National Life agents to submit an application through a Straight Through Process (STP)and is fully supported by both underwriting engines and a designated service team. It was a collaborative effort driven by the excitement and understanding that the team was creating something revolutionary.

> *A company is only as good as its people; so for a company to be recognized as best, it has to be filled with people committed to innovation, people committed to doing things better.*

The system allows National Life to move an application from agent submission to policy issue in less than two hours. No other company in the industry hosts such a system. The system reduces business cycle time. It also provides National Life associates with more time to dedicate to the customer experience and the kind of critical thinking that will help National Life continue to differentiate and innovate beyond their competitors.

NATIONAL LIFE HAS A DEEP HISTORY OF THIS.

As one of the original inventors of living benefits which allow you to access the money in your life insurance policy if you're diagnosed with a chronic, critical, or terminal illness, National Life has been an innovator in the industry since the company's beginning. In addition, the founders of National Life were innovators who created one of the very first mutual life insurance companies in the country— the first with a national vision.

The company's first death claim—that of Rowland Allen, who died in 1850 while seeking fortune in the California Gold Rush—pushed the company to its limits. The young company did not have the assets to pay the claim but the directors knew their company's future was doomed if they failed to pay. With the cooperation of a local bank and the personal credit backing of the directors, National Life came up with the money. Its President and Founder Dr. Julius Dewey personally delivered the $1,000 payment to the grieving but grateful widow.

Even today employees are proud to reflect upon their history and be a part of continuing the legacy. They want to be a part of doing better. Matt Frazee, Vice President and Controller, told us:

> *National Life's culture is unique. We are rooted in tradition, with over 167 years of history and credibility in doing the right thing. Egos tend to be small, reflecting a bit of where we are located, so we've created an environment where it's more important to have the right people on the team vs. getting individual credit. Our focus is clearly on the future and how we will improve on what we've built. New ideas, products, and ways of doing things are viewed positively and encouraged. Good ideas get in front of key decision makers quickly and everyone has the chance to add value. At National Life, there are endless opportunities to make a difference and Do Good.*

This is what happens when your company starts with a noble, heroic cause. It unleashes talent and accelerates innovation because when people are engaged they think and act like owners of the business. They are not Dead People Working, they are motivated and alive at work.

PASSION IS OBVIOUS.

Today, the legacy of National Life's founders lives strong in the hearts and minds of its people. But their strength as a vibrant company comes from more than their history. It comes from their ability to lead today and plan for tomorrow. It comes from their deep-seated desire to be relevant today and prominent tomorrow.

Today they are recruiting to a compelling story. National Life is looking for people who get the "spirit" of the company. They invite potential employees to think beyond the job itself and they challenge everyone to think about the "why" behind their job. Today culture is the boss at National Life. People have the freedom and tools to call out colleagues when they are not living the values or practicing Servant Leadership and if they are holding back the culture.

The mission upon which the company was founded in 1848 lives on and is simple, "keeping our promises." ***Ask employees what the company's mission is and they can recite it because it's been woven into the fabric of the company.*** This is not just a quotable phrase that lives in the lobby. In our work with National Life we have experienced the passion that employees have to keep the legacy alive and accomplish the mission. The deep-seated desire to deliver on a promise is alive and well.

EVEN INDUSTRY OBSERVERS GET THE SENSE SOMETHING IS DIFFERENT AT NATIONAL LIFE.

Stephen Howard has spent 30 years keeping a close eye on the insurance industry as publisher of Broker World Magazine. Steve's job is to publish news about brokers and the life and health insurance companies they represent.

Steve says, "I've been in and out of more home offices than I can believe." And the reception he generally receives is cordial but wariness prevails. "Executives know I visit to sell ads for the magazine."

But he found something unique during his National Life visits. "Here, it was all about, 'What can we learn from this guy?'"

> *"When you work at National Life you are being of service."*

Over the last few years Steve's made connections at conventions and meetings with CEO, Mehran Assadi and Executive Vice President, Ruth Smith. "We spent a lot of time talking and Mehran asked me to visit National Life campuses and sit down with several different department heads just to give them my take on brokerage, the important things to do, just share my experiences," Steve said.

After visiting both the Montpelier and Dallas campuses and getting to know the people and the culture of National Life, Steve has become one of National Life's biggest cheerleaders.

"I get the feeling that there's an undercurrent of service here," he said. "And I don't mean that forced smile on your face when you give somebody a burger and fries. I mean an undercurrent that says, 'when you work at National Life you are being of service.'"

WHATEVER-IT-TAKES.

In addition to bringing in industry representatives to share insights and experiences, National Life is doing whatever-it-takes on the inside to equip people at all levels with the information and resources they need to make good business decisions and offer great service.

The ability to deliver on their promises today and well into the future means everyone needs to be business literate and National Life is paving the way.

National Life
Group®

Understanding the Bottom Line
2013 Net Income

The way **National Life Group** makes money through the sale of life insurance, annuities, mutual funds and investment advisory and administrative services. We then take the money we receive from premiums, commissions and fees and invest it so we can grow it to pay benefits.

How We Make Money (Total Revenue)

Net Investment Income
While the company is holding the money, it is invested, producing investment income and capital gains.

Premiums
Policyholders give us cash in return for the promise of future benefits.

Policy and Contract Charges
We charge policyholders a fee for the cost of insurance and to cover policy maintenance and administration.

Mutual Fund Commission and Fee Income
We earn money for providing asset management, financial planning and investment products and services.

Other Income
Various other ways we earn money.

TOTAL REVENUE

Our Expenses (Offsetting Revenue)
Offsetting revenue are the many expenses we incur in the course of doing business. The company's expenses fall into two categories:

Policy Related Expenses
Our cost to acquire policies.

Commissions
The net amount (money after taxes) we pay our sales force for selling our policies.

Sales Costs
Accounting rules let us take the cost of putting a new policy on the books (i.e., commissions, underwriting, setup, administration) and set it aside to be expensed later when the policy is generating profits.

Operating Expenses

National Life designed a fun and simple profit and loss (P&L) statement to help all National Life stakeholders make good business decisions and more fully understand what impacts the bottom line.

The company isn't trying to turn every stakeholder into a financial whiz, but it does want everyone to have enough grasp of financial information to improve the quality and speed with which decisions are made. To draw people into the document, they've communicated the P&L in an interesting, fun, and relevant way. The packaging makes it compelling to read and the simplicity makes it easy to understand.

National Life recognizes that the true experts in any organization are those who are closest to the customer or the point of action.

When they engage—heart, mind, and soul—in the success of the business, they will come up with new ways to generate revenue and contain cost that others never thought of.

What's the alternative? Apathy? Unimaginative workers who are bored out of their minds? Business-as-usual? Dead people working?

National Life wants everyone to be engaged in growing the business and that means everyone has to have a sense of how the company makes a buck.

We sacrifice our deepest desires on the altar of "just getting by" and every time we do...we die a little bit inside.

PASSION ERUPTS WHEN WORK BECOMES A JOYOUS EXPRESSION OF THE SOUL.

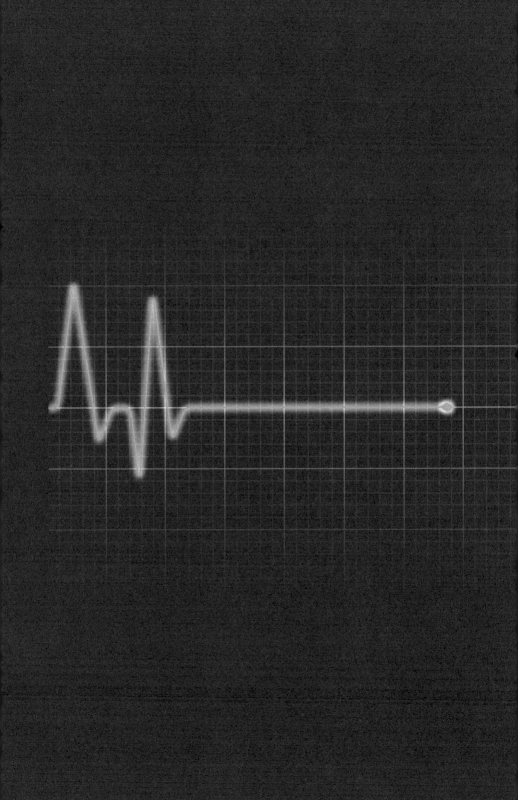

WHAT'S KILLING PEOPLE?
A CULTURE THAT SUCKS

A culture that sucks the life, passion, and energy out of people. People are dead because the places where they work lack interest, audacity, imagination, and zeal. Too many of us are working in companies that are sucking the passion, energy, and enthusiasm out of us by the hour.

These days it's very unusual for an outsider to ask: "What is it about your work environment that makes people so passionate about coming to work? How do you keep people so engaged, customers so loyal, and competitors so worried?"

In most organizations there's nothing about the culture worth asking about. If no one is breaking down the door, trying to find out what makes people remarkably different, is it any wonder?

THE AVERAGE CORPORATE CULTURE IS, WELL, JUST AVERAGE.

Stagnant work. Ask your friends, "What's new and exciting at work? What amazing things are you doing? What really cool problems are you working on now?" You're likely to get a lot of blank stares. People "flatline" because of the boredom, meaninglessness, and sense of futility they have at work. The Dead Sea got its name for a reason: it's stagnant, nothing lives there. The same could be said for work in many places.

Complacent leaders. No one is completely content with stagnant work and an uninspiring culture, but when was the last time you saw an impassioned leader throw down the gauntlet in outrage at the waste of human talent? When was the last time you heard an executive ask, "Are we worthy of the loyalty we desire? Do we have a culture that deserves the very best gifts and talents our people can bring to the game? Do we merit the outpouring of passion, ingenuity, initiative, and commitment we need to grow the business?"

A culture that sucks. Stagnant work. Complacent leaders. The effect is disastrous because people lose their hearts, suppress their dreams, lower their expectations, and abandon all hope for a sense of adventure. Then, resignation sets in.

SUBMISSIVE RESIGNATION IS SLOWLY KILLING PEOPLE AT WORK.

Trying to make ends meet or maintain their standard of living, many people are simply okay with just getting by—until they wake up and find that resignation has turned to regret.

Ours is a very special profession. People look to us to help them prepare for an unknown future. Whether it is economic challenges or life unexpected, we provide solutions that offer assurance for a better tomorrow.

Mehran Assadi

"GETTING BY." ARE YOU KIDDING? THAT'S NOT WHAT WE WERE MADE FOR!

We were made to use the gifts and talents that were planted in us for noble, worthy purposes. We were made to experience nothing less than LIFE at work and LIFE while living.

IT'S TIME TO STOP SACRIFICING OUR DESIRE FOR LIFE ON THE ALTAR OF JUST "GETTING BY."

DON'T LET RESIGNATION KILL YOU.

National Life does not tolerate resignation. This company is committed to creating a workplace were everyone, everywhere, every day feels valued, adds value, and lives the values.

In its ongoing quest to be an employer of choice, National Life's company culture is built around the tenets of Servant Leadership—respect, integrity, trust, passion, and service. The culture is grounded in more than 167 years of leadership and service to millions of policy holders and thousands of advisors and employees.

National Life is on a journey to help all employees and partners fully understand the importance of what they do. They don't make computers, cars, or widgets. They make promises! Their job is to deliver on those promises 10, 20, 50 years down the road.

Iola Carusi bought a National Life Insurance Company policy on October 12, 1929, just three weeks before the nation's first and most historic stock market crash. Iola was 19 years old. In December 2010, with her eyes bright and her smile strong, she turned 100 years old. National Life's relationship with Iola has spanned more than 80 years.

What other business can claim an ongoing, 80-year relationship of trust and service with a customer?

Today National Life employs over 1,000 people and partners with over 16,000 advisors. The company is committed to offering ongoing growth, development, and learning opportunities through National Life University. In 2014 National Life U offered 412 sessions of 114 courses which over 4,000 people attended. Learning and development is a key to enabling, empowering, and engaging people at all levels.

Tips for getting the most out of National Life Group's culture

1. Participate in the employee activities offered on both campuses

2. Take an exercise class or workout in the gym

3. Attend a Lunch and Learn offered by NLGroup University

4. Lunch with a co-worker outside your own working group

5. Participate in the volunteer program

6. Join a company committee or a group like Toastmasters

7. Participate in the alternative transportation program

8. Live our values — out loud!

LIVE OUR VALUES OUT LOUD!

Look for the green megaphones on the desks of Values In Action (VIA) ambassadors. They're dedicated to help you thrive in National Life Group's culture!

PASSPORT

Experience National Life Group's Culture

In addition, National Life understands the value of gaining input from all people. For more than 5 years employees have had an opportunity to voice their opinions about the company through an annual Pulse Survey focusing on three major areas:

• Goal Alignment
• Employee Engagement
• One Company—One Culture—One Message/Cause

This confidential 27-question survey is one more attempt to measure progress toward National Life's goal of creating a culture where everyone…

• Adds Value,
• Feels Valued, and
• Lives the Values.

And most recently in 2015, National Life deployed the Gallup Q12 to all employees in its quest to deeply root their corporate commitment to employee engagement.

In addition, National Life leaders participate in a cross-evaluation process, the evaluation provides 360-degree reliable data and transparency for advancing the practice of Servant Leadership. The process is designed to increase self-awareness by helping leaders better understand their impact on others.

> *We want every associate to have the opportunity to develop his or her skill, be mentored by caring and competent managers, provide and receive meaningful input and feedback, work on exciting strategic initiatives, and be fully engaged in building their own career. We want employment here to be much more than "just a job," we want it to be a creative, restorative, challenging, and inspiring experience.*
>
> **Ruth Smith**
> Executive Vice President

Eric Sandberg

At National Life, we witnessed a humbling example of saying NO to "just getting by," an example of a culture where employment can be restorative, challenging, and inspiring.

During an all employee workshop on culture and leadership, Eric Sandberg, National Life, Senior Vice President Chief Actuary and Chief Risk Officer, shared his personal story of career development, noting the value of feedback and self-awareness. Eric described an experience he had while working with an executive coach, noting that the coaching journey helped him better understand his impact on others. His coach suggested he follow-up with his peers and direct reports.

What about you...Do you need to say NO to "just getting by?"

So Eric crafted and sent a "thank you" email to his peers and direct reports. He thanked them for participating in his leadership assessment process and giving him a new perspective on his leadership development goals. And then Eric took the journey a step further and decided to share his thank you email at the all employee workshop. By being vulnerable to the entire organization and by sharing his experience with confident humility Eric's offered National Life a timeless and timely example of Servant Leadership.

THE REMEDY
BE A SOURCE OF INSPIRATION

I think many in the financial services industry aged 10 years during 2008. We faced an economic tsunami that none of us had ever experienced or even thought possible. Many saw their retirement dreams dashed. This very real and very raw experience is slow to heal.

> *Now we are in the midst of a retirement bubble; there are 78 million baby boomers focusing on their retirement plans. With the leading edge of boomers now in their 60s, and many in their 50s, they are doing all that they can to recoup their losses—and find safe havens for their protection and retirement dollars. And that brings them to us—offering strength, stability, and solutions for 167 years. Let's never forget, we offer what people want: A safe and secure haven in unpredictable times.*
>
> **Mehran Assadi**

Inspiration! We look for it in every leader and every leader looks for it in the people he or she leads.

Winston Churchill rallied a nation with it. In 1940 the Nazi juggernaut lurked over the horizon. Hitler had already overrun Austria, Czechoslovakia, France, Belgium, and Holland, and he was now threatening Russia. England would be next. But, in that dark and dangerous hour a hopeful and defiant attitude took hold as Churchill's words were broadcast across the free world:

> *We shall not flag or fail… We shall fight in France, we shall fight on the seas and oceans, we shall fight with growing confidence and growing strength in the air, we shall defend our Island, whatever the cost may be, we shall fight on the beaches, we shall fight on the landing grounds, we shall fight on the fields and in the streets, we shall fight in the hills; we shall never surrender!*

The House of Commons thundered in an uproar at his stirring rhetoric. Had Churchill not been able to see beyond the dark clouds of war, had he not demonstrated the courage to inspire a nation, and had Hitler won the Second World War, the world we live in now would be a very different place.

Cynicism. Negativity. Doom and gloom. These are the enemies of the kind of ingenuity, hope, and perseverance that will differentiate a company from the other players in its industry. To be a Great Company, a BEST place where the BEST people can do their BEST work to make the world BETTER you need:

LEADERS WHO CAN INSPIRE.
LEADERS WHO CAN WAKE THE DEAD PEOPLE WORKING!

When it comes to inspiring a movement, here's the thing. There has to be something so alive in you that it awakens something in others. When people bump into you, what spills out?

A HIGHER CALLING?
A COMMITMENT TO A CAUSE?
AN INVITATION TO CHANGE THE WORLD?
A SERVANT LEADERSHIP BRAND?

PEOPLE FOLLOW PASSION.

National Life is looking for leaders who want to build a Servant Leadership brand, a brand of infectious enthusiasm that draws and enlists people into something bigger. Something that is worthy of their time and talent. They're looking for leaders who want to reclaim the moral high ground by building a business around what Plato called the GOOD, the JUST, and the BEAUTIFUL.

NATIONAL LIFE IS COMMITTED TO THEIR OWN MORAL HIGH GROUND, "DO GOOD, BE GOOD, AND MAKE GOOD."

Simplicity proved inspirational. Even after getting some grief from senior leaders on the interpretation of their values: Do Good, Be Good, and Make Good. To some "Good" seemed to imply that they were settling for good vs. excellent or great. Despite the concern, Mehran was convinced it was the right thing to do.

HIS END GOAL WAS FOR THIS TO SERVE AS A GUIDEPOST FOR:

- Intention (Do Good)
- Action (Be Good)
- Outcome (Make Good)

Years later, at their annual Do Good Fest hosted on their corporate campus in Montpelier, Vermont, Tracy King wore the values with pride painted on her face for all other music festival attendees to see and a photographer captured the image. People fell in love with the picture. It resonated with something deep. It expressed their WHY. It instantly brought the company values to life and today Do Good, Be Good and Make Good is a National Life badge of honor. People want to be Do Gooders.

The Do Good Fest has become an annual Vermont summer tradition. In 2015 over 3,000 people attended the Do Good Fest which featured O.A.R., The Alternate Routes, Panama Wedding, Patti Casey, and Colin McCaffrey. The concert raised $15,000 for Branches of Hope, a cancer patient fund, and shined light on many other non-profits in the community.

Only six words. Six words that the people of National Life use as guiding principles in all they do, whether it is helping to do good through their charitable foundation, being good at what they do to provide the most comprehensive and competitive products for clients, or making good on a promise, these values are the foundation of the company's Servant Leadership culture.

In their 2014 Corporate Social Responsibility Report (CSR), there are countless examples of how they Do Good, Be Good and Make Good to enrich the culture of the company, the environment, the communities, the people, and the future.

Whether grounded on a Main Street or Wall Street, global concerns are top of mind for companies at large.

As their CSR report demonstrates, sustainability is a part of the DNA of National Life. Whether it's their commitment to investing in affordable housing, solar projects, LEED Certification, or recycling and more, the ongoing sustainability projects these people get behind are making the world better.

We at National Life are committed to a sustainable workplace by reducing our environmental impacts, educating our people, promoting our environmental programs, and creating a healthy work environment for this generation and future generations to come.

Tim Shea
Assistant Vice President
Facilities, Purchasing and Contracting

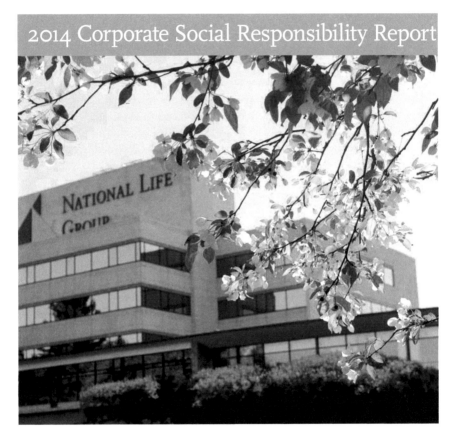

2014 Corporate Social Responsibility Report

Culture | Environment | Community | People | Future

Learn more about how the people of National Life Do Good through all of their CSR activities use the QR code on page 114.

Every year the people of National Life donate supplies, lend countless hands, raise money, and volunteer countless hours all in the spirit of Do Good and give back.

Assurance is a powerful cause. And what's also impressive is the number of people at National Life who get involved in making today and tomorrow better. In addition to delivering on business promises, they are also good stewards of our natural resources. The people of National Life unselfishly invest their time and talents so generations to come can also experience a more global assurance—the ability to live, work, and play in an environment that is good for them.

PART 6
FIGHTING FOR A NOBLE, HEROIC CAUSE

WILL WORK FOR A CAUSE.

A leader who dismisses as irrelevant our needs for heroism, meaning, belonging, and living lives that matter is, in a sense, rejecting our humanity. The rejection tells us to bring only a certain part of ourselves to work every day—the part that wants a paycheck. Leaders who are intellectually and emotionally insensitive to these needs depreciate the intellectual, physical, and emotional capital that is critical to their success.

But, if you can convince people that there is something about their work that has eternal significance, you can awaken their hearts and minds. If you can realistically convince people that their work has meaning beyond their daily routines, you can begin to draw out of them some deeply rooted, life-inspiring passions.

> *Do you want to spend the rest of your life selling sugared water, or do you want a chance to change the world?*
>
> *Steve Jobs inviting John Sculley to be the CEO of Apple*

The gutsiest leaders in history—Jesus, Gandhi, Joan of Arc, Rosa Parks, Martin Luther King, and Mother Teresa, to name a few—did not set out to become world-renowned leaders. They set out to pursue a cause so compelling and so powerful that others got caught up in the movement. Their passion to address a need and create a better world captivated people's hearts and minds, drawing them to make personal and professional sacrifices for the good of the cause. These leaders believed in their causes so deeply that their faith ignited the power and potential of those around them.

A CAUSE IN BUSINESS CAN DO THE SAME THING!

The idea is to satisfy peoples' deep-seated hunger for meaning and their desire to live a life that matters. National Life is a community of people grounded in Good. A glance back in time proves they've played a crucial role in an epic story—a story pioneered in 1848. A story that they can add to, a story where personal contributions are valued and peace of mind prevails.

If you talk to the people of National Life you quickly get a sense that they feel a sense of joy in and responsibility for continuing this story. After an all employee leadership workshop in Dallas, Cindy Duck shared her joy in working for National Life. Cindy's job is to deal with "escalated" problems and find solutions, but listen to how she describes what she does:

> *I do love what I do here at National Life. It is a great company to work for. I started in licensing but when an Agent Services Advisor job came along I took it and I love what I do. I work with our Agents, Regional VPs, and Independent Marketing Organizations. I take escalations (AKA problems) and try to find the issue and make it all better.*

WHEN YOU BELIEVE YOUR WORK MATTERS THREE THINGS WILL HAPPEN:

First, you will unlock a vast treasure chest of passion, commitment, determination, ingenuity, and energy—things customers and advisors enjoy and competitors will find very difficult to replicate.

Second, the organization will become a powerful magnet for extraordinary talent—people will beat down the doors to get in.

Third, you will give history a shove!

WHERE TO START?
DEFINE THE BUSINESS AS A CAUSE.
LEARN TO TELL THE STORY WELL.
INVITE PEOPLE TO JOIN THE MOVEMENT.

PRESERVING PEOPLE'S MEMORIES

Several years ago we led a seminar that was attended by people who worked in one-hour photo shops. We asked everyone in the room,

WHAT'S HEROIC ABOUT WHAT YOU DO?

There were a lot of answers: We exceed our customers' expectations. The clarity of our prints is unmatched. Customers can count on the reliability and speed of our service.

Finally, a woman in the back of the room stood up and said, "That's all true, but it isn't heroic. Our work is heroic because we preserve people's memories—the birth of a child, a wedding, an exotic vacation. We capture some of the most important times of people's lives."

THERE WAS A MOMENT OF SILENCE.

Then a murmur of excitement coursed through the room. We could feel the level of energy and engagement rise. She got it right.

What ignites enthusiasm and inspires performance more: saying that you process film and paper better than anyone else, or saying that you capture the moments that make life rich and interesting?

Suddenly, these photo processors had a cause that put their work into a larger context, one that made a positive contribution to the world. What had been an advertising slogan was suddenly a reality in their lives, something that gave their work meaning and significance.

TAKE IT FROM TOM MORRIS AUTHOR OF,
IF ARISTOTLE RAN GENERAL MOTORS:

> *Every job productive of any good can be given either a trivial description or a noble description. Ultimate motivation requires that we have in our minds a noble description of what we do!*

By defining your business in heroic terms you are giving your people a focus, a beacon, and a cause that puts their sometimes-humdrum daily work into a larger, ennobling perspective.

A CAUSE BUILT ON TIMELESS PRINCIPLES

What are the big ideas that get a lot of airtime in most companies? Shareholder return. Supply chain efficiency. Cost containment. Discipline. Accountability. Execution. All are critical to a successful business, but do they speak to your heart? Do they open the floodgates of adrenaline? Do they say anything about meaning and significance?

Now think about some of the global leaders who have inspired you. Nelson Mandela. Melinda Gates. Steve Jobs. Richard Branson. Desmond Tutu. Malala Yousafzai. Bono. Muhammad Yunus. Rick Warren. Jeff Bezos. Lift the hood and look at the values that inspired these leaders. Their extraordinary achievements were driven by an unwavering commitment to the timeless principles of...

FAITH. HOPE. LOVE. TRUTH. JUSTICE. FREEDOM. BEAUTY.

Aren't these the ideals we aspire to most as human beings? These are the very ideals born on Main Street, ignited by a handshake, and empowered through community and relationships. When we encounter them don't they raise our pulse and quicken our step? These are the things we live for. These are the things we can't live without.

Why then is the language of business so devoid of these enduring principles? How is it that business leaders craft mission, vision, and purpose statements that are so mechanistic, sterile, and uninspiring, and then they wonder why we have so many dead people working? What if we could define our business in terms of a noble, heroic cause infused with our highest ideals—a cause that speaks to our hearts and makes us speak passionately about what we do?

In the movie, Dead Poets Society, John Keating, played by Robin Williams, is the English teacher who brings his unconventional teaching methods to a very traditional all-boys school. On the opening day of class Keating conveys his outrage and contempt for those who objectify poetry.

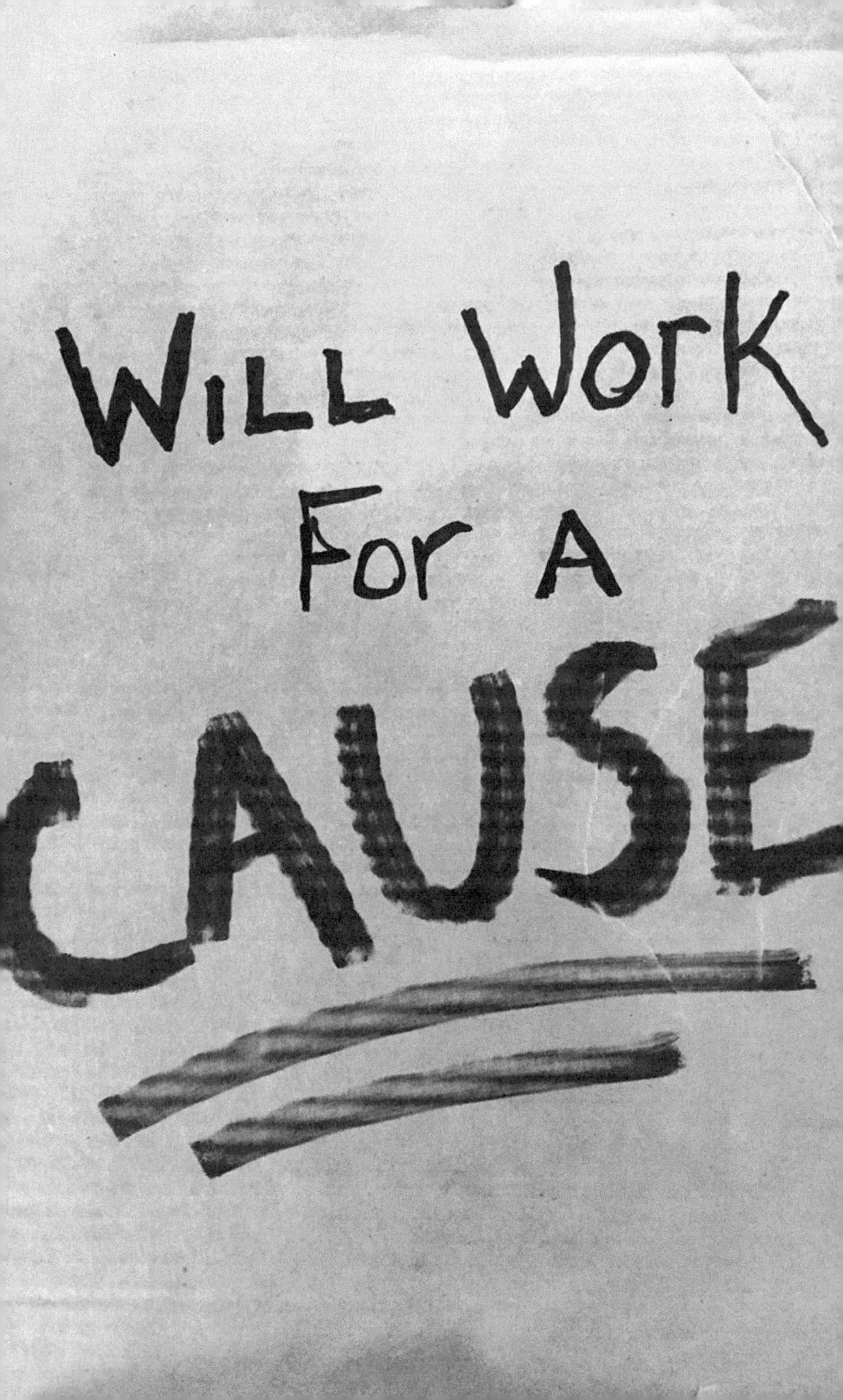
WILL WORK
FOR A
CAUSE

In a scene from the film you can see how the passion and infectious enthusiasm of an insanely great leader commands the students' attention and captivates their interest in a subject many of them thought irrelevant. As Keating stoops low and draws the boys into a huddle, he says,

> *We don't read and write poetry because it's cute. We read and write poetry because we are members of the human race. And the human race is filled with passion. And medicine, law, business, engineering—these are noble pursuits and necessary to sustain life. But poetry, beauty, romance, love— these are what we stay alive for.*

Imagine sharing and engaging in a cause that is founded on passion, love, truth service, and justice. How about a cause that calls forth courage and perseverance, demands a maniacal focus, fosters a revolutionary spirit, and gives people hope for a better world?

WOULD YOU SIGN UP TO WORK FOR SUCH A CAUSE?

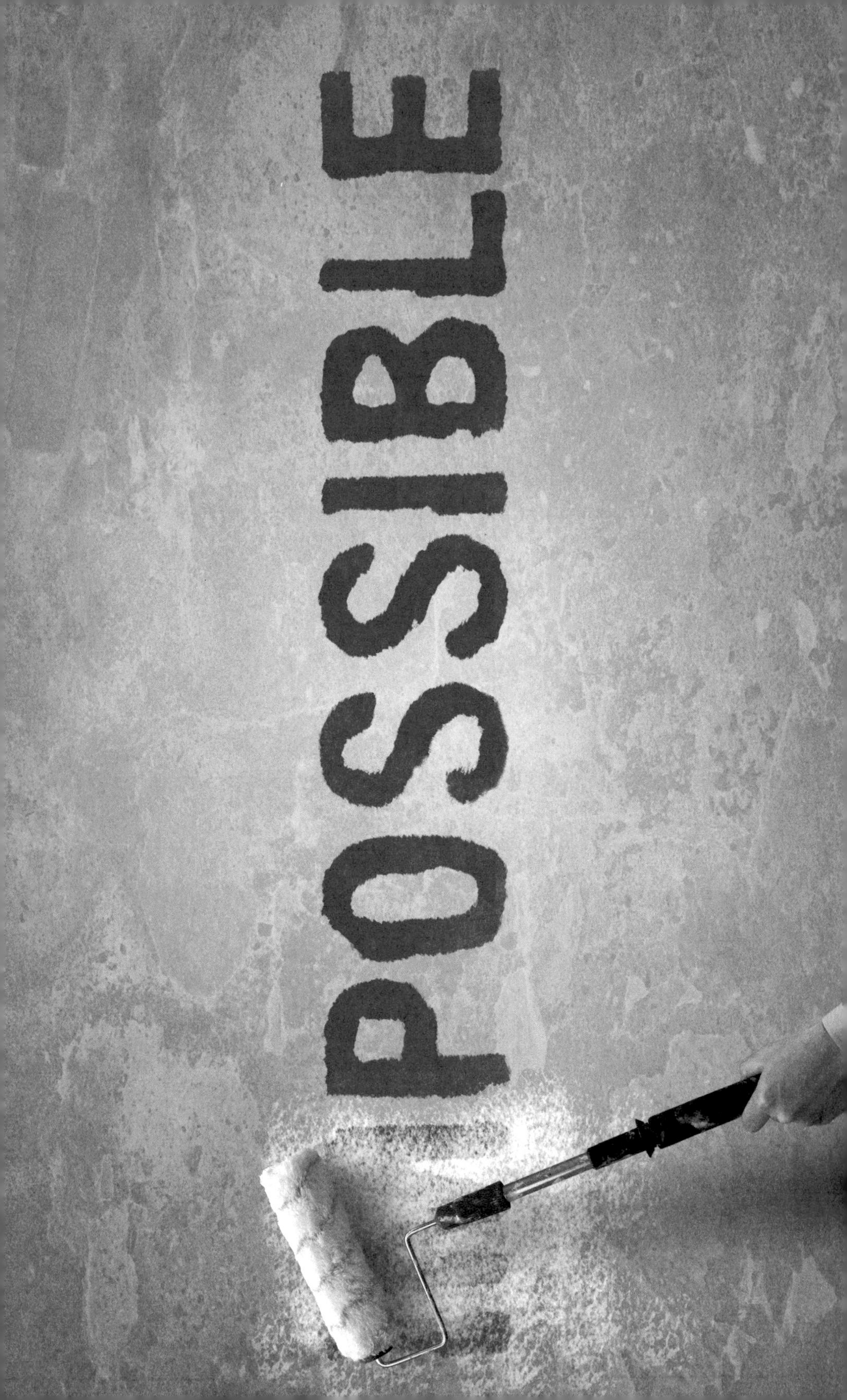
POSSIBLE

WE GIVE OUR LIVES TO A CAUSE, NOT A JOB

We all want to believe in what we do.

IS THERE SOME INDIGNITY OUT THERE THAT IS CALLING YOU?

WHAT IMPOSSIBLE DREAM HAS YOUR NAME ON IT?

These are the questions from which legends and legacies are made.

Most of us don't lay down our lives for a job, but we will for a cause that is heroic. If you held a job that conflicted with your deepest values or, in your view, contributed little to the world, would you give your heart and soul to your work? Probably not. You'd go through the motions, get through the day, and live for the important things outside of work.

People don't give their all to make budget or quarterly numbers, but they will for an opportunity to make a difference, to fulfill a dream, to enrich a life.

THINK ABOUT A TIME IN YOUR LIFE WHEN YOU WORKED ON A REALLY COOL PROJECT. WHAT WAS IT ABOUT THIS PROJECT THAT MADE YOU COME ALIVE?

Was it the opportunity to blaze a new trail, to do something innovative and unprecedented? Was it the boldness and daring needed to take on the project? Was it working with creative people who shared the same dream? Were you solving a problem that really matters? Were you designing something to enrich lives?

WHAT IF YOU COULD REPLICATE THE ENTHUSIASM AND JOY, DISCIPLINE AND COMMITMENT, AND INITIATIVE AND INGENUITY FROM THAT SCENARIO?

What if you could identify a problem so large in scope that it required major chutzpa? What if it was a truly a noble undertaking?

THE NATIONAL LIFE LEGACY REQUIRED MAJOR CHUTZPA.

Consider National Life Insurance Company's Founder and first President, Dr. Julius Dewey. Dr. Dewey, now considered a pioneer of the industry, embarked upon a noble undertaking, an undertaking that required thick skin and great courage.

PEACE OF MIND

As a concerned country doctor he felt called to protect people from the long-term consequences of unexpected, heartbreaking circumstances. In 1848 on horseback, he traveled from town to town sharing the value of life assurance while building lasting relationships one person at a time.

Talk to anyone in the National Life community and you quickly get a sense of destiny. They believe a baton has been passed down through the corridors of history and on to them. They have a legacy to uphold:

For the people and partners of National Life this is their calling. This is their noble undertaking. This is their WHY.

Life Assurance—bringing peace of mind to everyone we touch by delivering on our promises year after year, through the Civil War, the great flu epidemic of 1918, the Great Depression, two World Wars and most recently, the Great Recession.

What if you found a solution to a problem and changed the world? What if you could be a part of transforming lives? What if all this came together in a community bound together by shared values and an aspiration for enriching lives—a community in which you knew you belonged?

You'd become an impassioned person who gets out of bed every morning fully awake, fully alive, and firing on all cylinders.

AND, YOU'D PROBABLY NEVER WORK ANOTHER DAY IN YOUR LIFE! WHAT IF YOUR WORK BECOMES YOUR CALLING?

The people of National Life respond to problems every day—it's their job. What makes working in a call center so special, what gets customer service agents out of bed, what puts a spring in their step? Knowing their "why." Like Cindy Duck said, "I try to find their issue and make it all better."

Check out a day in the LIFE of the National Life Customer Service Department:

A policy owner in his early 60s called the customer service desk. He explained he had a life insurance policy and asked if he could accelerate his death benefit rider. After the rep confirmed his policy, she said she would be happy to help but needed to know what type of issue he had that created the need to trigger this rider.

A DAY IN
THE LIFE OF THE
NATIONAL LIFE
CUSTOMER
SERVICE
DEPARTMENT

He explained he was just diagnosed with terminal cancer and was given six months to live. He wanted to quickly book a cruise and take his entire family with him so they could make some lasting memories while they still could.

Within a week, his check was processed.

One of National Life's agents strongly encouraged his grandson to buy a life insurance policy. His grandson wasn't convinced; he was in his early 20s and there were many other uses for his money. But his grandfather was insistent that it was the right thing to do. His grandson finally agreed and purchased a policy from National Life.

About two years later, the grandson was diagnosed with a rare form of cancer. His prognosis was grim but after exploring all options, he discovered an experimental treatment in Germany for his type of cancer that wasn't offered in the United States.

He called the customer service center and explained his situation. He asked to accelerate his critical death benefit rider so he could use the money to go to Germany for treatment. His request was processed and last we heard he was doing well.

A woman in her late 50s was diagnosed with MS. After a few years, she became wheelchair bound and her adult daughter spent more and more time helping her while working part-time.

> *I try to find their issue and make it all better.*
>
> *Cindy Duck*

As time went on, the daughter was torn. She needed her paycheck but also wanted to help her mother whose health was deteriorating. She had a heart-to-heart with her mother and shared her dilemma.

The next day the mother called the customer service department and asked if she could accelerate her chronic illness rider. The answer was yes. The mother did just that and used the money from her policy to pay her daughter who then quit her job and spent her time caring for her mother.

Imagine the routine of answering the phone, processing a check, accelerating a rider—all jobs that need to get done. Right? Nope, these aren't jobs... these are real people with lives they want to live. And the people at National Life truly believe that their job is to "make it all better."

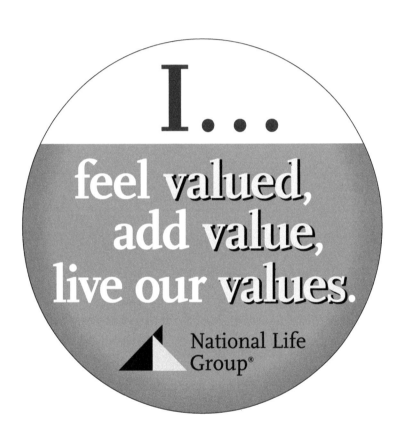

When we met with Mehran during a marketing meeting in San Diego, he was reflective in his description of National Life. He said, "Our leaders show up different today. We are not a command and control culture any more. Today we are building a culture of innovators and Servant Leaders who add value, feel valued, and live our values every day."

People are capable of the highest generosity and self-sacrifice. But they have to feel and believe that what they are doing is truly…heroic, timeless, and supremely meaningful.

The crisis of modern society is precisely that people no longer feel heroic.

Ernest Becker
The Denial of Death

WHAT IS YOUR WHY?

KNOW YOUR WHY

Building a business that boldly separates itself from the sea of sameness in any industry requires personal conviction, thick skin, and resilience. These character strengths require a sense of destiny compelling enough to resist the gravitational pull of the things—fear, inertia, and resistance—that stand in the way of your success.

Why do we exist?

Why is that important?

Why is the world better because of us?

What consequential, awe-inspiring problem are we trying to solve?

If we disappeared from the face of the earth tomorrow, why would we be missed?

THESE ARE THE QUESTIONS THAT MUST BE ANSWERED WHEN YOU DEFINE A BUSINESS AS A CAUSE.

When the answers are crystal clear, people have a laser-like focus on what they are trying to accomplish. They don't easily waver in the face of adversity because they know their "WHY." And their "WHY" is extremely compelling.

WHY INSPIRES ENGAGEMENT.

Cause-oriented companies inspire people to engage. There is no manipulation. That means people give themselves to the work because they want to, not because they have to.

In cause-oriented companies motivation is internal. People bring their best selves to the game because it's intrinsically rewarding to do so, not because they'll earn an award, a pin, a trip, a promotion, or the next level of compensation.

The incentive to act isn't temporary and superficial; it's deeply personal because the cause represents their own values and expresses their own inner passions. Material rewards are the icing on the cake, the "nice to have" symbols of hard work, and the company's appreciation for major accomplishments. But the cool "stuff" isn't what keeps us in the game for the long haul.

What frustrates you?
What makes your blood boil?
What makes you feel indignant?
What gets your creative juices flowing?

There is a cause out there with your name on it, something you care about deeply. It doesn't just present itself to you. You have to look for it. When you see it you have to go get it.

AND WHEN YOU FIND IT...YOU WILL HAVE A COMPELLING REASON TO GET OUT OF BED IN THE MORNING.

WHAT IS YOUR "WHY"?

For the people of National Life it's assurance to seniors wanting financial independence at retirement and beyond, assurance in the event of a chronic illness or serious injury, assurance to small businesses in the event of an economic downturn, or assurance to a family who unexpectedly lost a loved one.

This is what Mehran recently stated in his 2015 forecast for *Broker World* Magazine,

> *As our focus has shifted from death benefits to living benefits, we can truly say that we are all about life assurance.*

> *As an industry and as a society we have underplayed and underappreciated what National Life provides today to individuals, to families, and to our nation.*

> *Our benefits are no longer just paid out after a policy holder has died. Our benefits today are for the living. We insure people's lives while they are alive. We are helping people through illness; we provide streams of income when they're needed.*

Perhaps your cause is radically different. But make no mistake there is a cause out there with your name on it, something you care about deeply. It doesn't just present itself to you. You have to look for it. When you see it go for it.

WHEN YOU FIND YOUR WHY, YOU FIND YOUR WAY.

WHEN THE BUSINESS
BECOMES A CAUSE
WHAT FOLLOWS
IS A MOVEMENT

PART 7
JOIN THE MOVEMENT

A GOOD UPRISING GETS THE ADRENALINE PUMPING.

When the business becomes a cause, what follows is a movement. When you define your life and work in terms of a noble, heroic cause, something very exciting happens. You will never have to ask, "Does my work matter?" You will know it matters because you will have a direct link from your individual contributions to something bigger, something deeply meaningful.

Rally a critical mass of people who think and act like this and you will have a movement in the making.

Conjure up your own images of the civil rights movement in the U.S., the movement to abolish apartheid in South Africa, or the Solidarity movement in Poland. What do these movements have in common?

They were born of intolerance, outrage, and an intense dissatisfaction with the present.

They demanded self-sacrifice and single-hearted allegiance.

Members of the movement were either ignorant of or impervious to the obstacles that stood in their way—they didn't know they couldn't do it.

A healthy level of fanaticism and a fervent hope for the future sustained the movement.

People gained a sense of purpose, confidence, and belonging by identifying themselves with the efforts and achievements of the movement.

Our forefathers viewed life insurance as life assurance. I love what Benjamin Franklin once said: "A policy of life assurance is the cheapest and safest mode of making provision for one's family." In the 167 years since the chartering of National Life Insurance Co., much has changed: Today we are known as National Life. We have added annuities and investments to our range of financial solutions. We have grown tremendously. In 1853 we hit the $1 million mark of insurance in-force. Today we have: $82 billion insurance in-force, $30 billion assets under management, 16,000 advisors and producers, and 390,000 promises in-force, and we are growing.

Unchanged, however, is the peace of mind our company and our industry delivers.

Our founders could not have imagined a world with paperless policies transmitted through the Internet and viewed on electronic tablets. But they would recognize our passion, our desire to keep alive the dreams of families, the hopes of small business owners, and the dignity and financial independence of seniors.

To them, like us, this is not a job. It is a calling. To them, like us, our cause is life assurance.

Mehran Assadi

Experience the cultures of Apple, Southwest Airlines, Zappos, Virgin, Whole Foods, Lululemon, Medtronic, and National Life. Something is going on in these companies beyond making computers; flying people from one point to another; selling shoes, healthy food, and yoga mats; manufacturing medical supplies; and selling financial services. You quickly get the sense that employees are caught up in something that transcends the bottom line.

The people in these companies believe that the products and services they provide have great social value. Their emotional connection with a larger cause unleashes a powerful flow of pride, passion, perseverance, and productivity.

When you listen to Mehran Assadi talk, you get a sense of why his revolutionary spirit, maniacal focus, missionary zeal, and upbeat attitude make National Life more like a crusade than a business.

MEHRAN SHARES HIS LOVE FOR THE CAUSE.

National Life Group® Do good.

CAUSE INSPIRES A MOVEMENT

From the outside looking in, it appears that when you join or partner with National Life you are stepping into a movement. The people you work with aren't just doing a job. They're engaging in a worthy cause. There is a healthy level of fanaticism, a fervent hope for the future, and an intense dissatisfaction with the status quo. These characteristics define the people and partners of National Life.

DON'T PITCH, ENRICH.

The people and partners at National Life don't pitch policies; they enrich lives one relationship at a time.

It sounds like "apple pie, puppy dogs and rainbows" to say that the products you are creating will bring peace of mind, but the people of National Life know it to be true—and that's what matters.

PEACE OF MIND AND ASSURANCE.

Ruth Smith sees peace of mind, dignity, and life assurance delivered regularly in her role as Executive Vice President.

> *I have the good fortune of working directly with our agents who offer protection solutions to clients if they die sooner or live longer than expected or become ill or injured. We are also a leader in providing living benefits to our policy holders by offering life insurance you don't have to die to use.*
>
> *My team and I have received many policy holder requests to access their living benefits for things like experimental medical treatments that might not be covered by their health plan, or assistance that will allow them to continue living in their homes while recovering from a critical illness.*
>
> *For years we've heard heartwarming stories about how a life insurance policy from a National Life company has helped a family or a business owner in the most difficult of times. My team and I are reinvigorated knowing that by keeping our promises to our policy holders we have made a positive difference in someone's life.*

FREE
ENTERPRISE
IS THE
AMERICAN
WAY

GOOD GLOBAL INVESTMENTS.

Tom Brownell, the Chief Investment Officer of National Life and CEO of the company's asset management firm, Sentinel Investments, said that the company's values are reflected in its investments.

We take to heart National Life's value to Do Good. The long-term needs of our policy holders must be the primary focus of our investments but within that philosophy we have the ability to do good throughout the nation, investing in our communities through affordable housing and solar projects and providing long-term capital for American businesses.

Additionally, when Andrew Boczek, a Sentinel Investment portfolio manager was asked to discuss performance, overall investment philosophy, and what contributes to attractive returns, he repeatedly referenced the value of good.

A good company is a good company is a good company. We continue to try to own businesses that should be resilient regardless of the macroeconomic circumstances. The companies we own have very strong balance sheets. So I think our underlying businesses should thrive regardless of the environment. If there's a recession or a crisis or something, are they going to suffer? Yes, but I think they're in good shape, relative to other companies out there.

EMPOWERING FREE ENTERPRISE.

NATIONAL LIFE IS ABOUT MAKING A PROFIT WHILE MAKING A DIFFERENCE.

While speaking to one of National Life's Independent Marketing Organizations (IMO) at a marketing conference in 2015, Mehran said, "Profitability is not a four letter word. Profitability allows us to offer fair deals to our clients, compensate our agents, and grow the capital of our company."

He is unapologetic, rightly so, about making money, while doing good for others.

Additionally, National Life is equipping a critical mass of agents and advisors to chart their own course in life and run their own successful businesses.

Career and General Agent, Jim Ortenzio, mentioned that 20 percent of National Life's new business is from the Asian markets. National Life is experiencing a big BOOM in the number of Chinese and Indian agents. Both represent communities with impressive work ethics and they fully embrace the idea of making a profit

while making a difference—doing something good for their families, their friends, and their extended communities.

Business opportunities, free enterprise, and entrepreneurship all pave the way toward affluence. When agents raise the standard of living and improve their own quality of life, these partners, in turn, create more jobs, pay more taxes, and give more back to the communities from which they take. And they all play a significant role in growing the economy.

National Life is committed to growing free enterprise. For example, in 2008 when the recession hit, National Life field leadership teams made it a primary focus to train and equip their advisors and independent marketing organizations on creative ways to build and grow their businesses despite the threatening economy.

More recently, National Life launched the Do Good Tour in 2014, a program designed to equip agents with a tent, banners, and National Life branded materials to use at festivals and major events in their communities. The intention is to help build business while also showing their Do Good spirit. For each Do Good Tour agents identify a local nonprofit that becomes the beneficiary of a donation from National Life's Foundation. Financial service products are not promoted at the Do Good Tours. The idea is to highlight the good agents do within the company and in their local communities.

National Life and their IMOs collectively celebrate diversity and empower leaders who want to make their families and communities better They are empowering women by bringing them into financial services and have established WIN (Women's Insight Network) which supports female agents. Together they are also introducing the concept of free enterprise and entrepreneurship to refugee communities here in the U.S. who want to achieve the American Dream And their networks are growing in Asian, African American and Hispanic communities as well.

We heard it mentioned over and over again: relationships drive our business. National Life and its IMOs broker products, but in their minds they build relationships first.

Victor Muro, a General Agent with National Life, has always been interested in helping people, whether it's helping his clients financially protect their families and futures or helping out his Staten Island, New York, community.

Derek Siver's Rendition on How to Create a Movement

Victor told us, "I witnessed many instances in which family members and friends suffered the profound consequences of poor life insurance and retirement planning, and wanted to prevent other people from experiencing the same kinds of difficulty."

One such person was Sharlene Nelson.

Almost twenty years ago, Victor provided business insurance for Sharlene's husband, Chris, and his partners. Sharlene remembers,

"I recall my husband at first, as well as the partners, resisting life insurance and disability insurance due to premiums. After much persistence with professional education and service, my husband and his partners finally listened and took the advice."

As time went on, Victor, Sharlene, and Chris maintained their professional relationship but also developed a strong friendship. Then Chris was diagnosed with cancer.

National Life and their IMOs are inspiring a movement one relationship, one friend, one family, one business at a time.

"We were emotionally devastated," said Sharlene. "From a financial standpoint we were covered. Our standard of living and cash flow didn't miss a beat…not to mention our life insurance premiums were now being paid by the life insurance company because of a special rider Victor put on the policy." Sharlene continued, "Less than two years later, I lost my husband, and my kids lost their father forever. Words can't express what we felt Thank God for Victor convincing my husband to purchase life insurance. Financially speaking, Vic delivered on the promises he made. My kids will be going to college; my mortgage is paid off; and a steady cash flow is coming in. I have little financial concerns now because of Vic Muro's professionalism and integrity."

"He came to the funeral, and checks in with my 17-year-old son Dylan as a friend and life mentor frequently, in addition to performing quarterly financial reviews for me. Victor Muro is 'financial integrity' and now a cherished friend for life."

Enriching lives. Restoring peace of mind. Keeping promises. Good global investing. Growing free enterprise. These pursuits inspire people to bring a maniacal focus and missionary zeal to life and work every day.

At National Life a movement is growing one relationship, one friend, one family, one business at a time.

If you haven't seen Derek Siver's rendition of how to create a movement in less than three minutes, this is a brilliant illustration of what we are talking about.

COMMITMENT
ARE YOU ALL IN?

MOVEMENTS = OPT-IN VS. BUY-IN

People OPT-IN to movements. They don't have to be manipulated or head locked into joining; they enlist themselves. They don't have to be bought—enticed with fancy cars, epic trips, or CPS (cheap plastic stuff) to sign up; they are already drawn to the psychic gratification, the deep meaning, and the significance they garner from solving a problem that matters, enriching lives, and providing peace of mind and assurance for life unexpected.

YOU DON'T HAVE TO "RECRUIT" THEM: THEY HAVE ALREADY BEEN RECRUITED BY THE CAUSE.

Let's get real. Building a business is extremely hard work. It's not enough to dream with great boldness. At some point you have to wake up and bust your butt to make that dream a reality. Fulfilling an audacious dream means you must be as bold and daring about realizing the dream as you are about the dream itself.

IT COMES FROM A 100 PERCENT, FULL-BLOWN COMMITMENT.

Buy-in is what would happen if, with self-serving motives, you were to embellish the National Life story simply to manipulate people into signing up. Commitment is not about pushing products and recruiting more salespeople because you want to "make the numbers."

Commitment is about opt-in. Opt-in happens when people are inspired by the significance of the story and the nobility of the cause. No one needs to be convinced; they can see themselves in the cause. No one needs to be motivated; they motivate themselves. No one needs to be micromanaged; they set their own rigorous targets. They opt-in because their personal values resonate with the values driving the movement. Commitment is about sharing benefits with friends, loved ones, and colleagues because you deeply believe in their value.

THERE IS NOTHING WRONG WITH BUY-IN UNLESS YOU ARE CONCERNED ABOUT RETENTION, SUSTAINED PRODUCTIVITY, AND BUILDING LIFELONG RELATIONSHIPS.

When people feel it is their duty or obligation to buy-in they are in it for the wrong reason; they won't last and your business will suffer.

WE DO SOMETHING THAT REALLY MATTERS, WE PROVIDE LIFE FOR MIDDLE AMERICA, EMPLOYING AND SERVING THE MOST UNDERSERVED PIECE OF THE INSURANCE MARKET.

Louis Puglisi

Yet, a movement inspires commitment; it causes people to say,

"I WANT IN! I WANT TO FIGHT FOR THIS CAUSE WITH YOU."

In Vermont we connected with Louis Puglisi, Senior Vice President, Protection and Retirement Distribution for National Life. We asked Louis to tell us about National Life. This is what he shared:

> We do something that really matters, we provide LIFE for Middle America, employing and serving the most underserved piece of the insurance market.

As a young boy Louis was inspired by his own father's example of investing in security instead of stuff. Louis has opted-in to a movement, he went on to say:

> National Life is a medium-size company with one campus headquartered in the hills of Vermont and another in the center of Texas, providing Middle America peace of mind and a path to affluence and security. We make life better. We make life livable. We manufacture products that matter in life not just at death. Our employees and our agents are the face of America—together we are National Life.

People who are committed bring a special energy, passion, and excitement to the game that cannot be manufactured. They might not have created the dream, but they become dreamers in the process because they identify with the cause and want the dream to be fulfilled as badly as the originators do.

Opting-in is about risk taking and putting it on the line. It's about going above and beyond the call of duty for a chance to make a difference. Buying-in is about taking orders. People who buy-in aren't self-starters. They don't initiate well. And they rarely make successful entrepreneurs.

WHEN THE CAUSE IS COMPELLING, IT FOSTERS A COVENANT THAT SAYS,

"We share a common purpose that I deeply believe in. Because of this, I will choose service over self-interest. I will serve the common good. I am committed to locking arms with you and doing WHATEVER IT TAKES to strengthen our movement. I'm all in."

Commitment means people live the Servant Leadership tenets because they want to, not because they have to.

装 修 期 間
照 常 營 業
Office Under renovation,
We Open everyday.

National Life Group
917-285-2850

The Audit Team, a team of "compliance" focused people, tackled this question, "What does a culture of Servant Leadership mean?"

After a collaborative meeting and some focused conversation, the Audit Team opted in by creating a word cloud as a daily reminder of how they will practice and live the National Life Servant Leadership tenets.

What brings you more assurance, commitment or obligation? We're betting on commitment.

Career and General Agent, Jim Ortenzio, also thinks National Life is America's best kept secret. Ortenzio shared the power of commitment among some agents in their New York office. The sign translated from Chinese to English illustrates the commitment he experienced when he showed up on December 26th during the holiday and while the office was under renovation.

Despite all the disruptions, this was the leading sales unit in all of National Life—an office filled with agents who are "all in."

Can you remember a time when something that was assigned to you brought you more joy and aliveness than something you chose to do?

Neither can we.

DISRUPT
THE
STATUS
QUO

ASSURANCE FANATICS
MEMBERS OF THE NATIONAL LIFE MOVEMENT

When you know you are connected to a community of people who are fighting for a noble cause, you're more willing to disrupt the status quo, even when everyone else in the industry might think you are nuts.

Early on in history National Life concluded that there is no better prescription for life or death unscripted than life insurance with a living benefits rider.

If you talk to the partners of National Life you quickly get a sense that they are fanatical about opting into this cause; they too are fueling the movement. They are keen on solving problems that really matter and so... their lives matter.

TO KNOW THAT OUR WORK COUNTS IS TO KNOW THAT WE COUNT.

David Carroll of Premier Financial Alliance (PFA), one of the largest independent marketing organizations working with National Life, told us, "We are on a crusade, a mission to educate Americans about life insurance with living benefits. What separates us from the competition? A relatively unknown set of insurance products that are the greatest financial products in the market today."

Carroll's passion is contagious; he wants Americans to be prepared for life unscripted.

The Alliance Group was the very first IMO to write a life insurance policy with living benefit riders as an independent agency through National Life in 1998.

Lee Duncan with Alliance Group told us, "Dreams, aspirations, goals are what we want to help clients accomplish and we don't want any unexpected situations to get in their way."

We also talked with Debbie and Phil Gerlicher, owners of First Financial Securities (FFS), another one of National Life's most successful independent marketing organizations (IMOs).

It doesn't take long to discover that the Gerlichers see their work as much more than a job. They're on a mission to care for, equip, and empower Middle America. This segment of the American population is vastly underserved and under-protected, living from paycheck to paycheck, accruing insurmountable debt and at risk of retiring without financial security, without dignity.

"National Life is a throwback to the GOOD old days, a business that is grounded in relationships and great products."

Debbie and Phil Gerlicher

We asked, "What is the appeal in partnering with National Life?" Their answer, "National Life is a throwback to the GOOD old days, a business that is grounded in relationships and great products (in that order)."

We live in a world in which the media is relentless in luring us into thinking we can have it all, we can have it now and deal with it later. Jimmy Buffet has a song that brings this to life.

According to Buffet we live in a world of temporary feelings that are always attached to permanent reminders—a tattoo that seemed like a good idea after a night of partying, hormones unchecked tonight then an unwanted pregnancy tomorrow, and a jacked up credit card today crashing your credit score for years to come. You get the point.

From what we've discovered, National Life agents and IMOs are fanatical and crusade-like in their dedication to empowering people to say NO to some of life's temporary pleasures in favor of a more dignified future.

IF **YOU** WORK
FOR A **CAUSE**
BIGGER THAN
YOURSELF
YOU WILL **WORK**
HARDER & SMARTER

MOVEMENT OR COMPANY?

How is National Life more like a movement than a "company"?

Well, first of all, they are empowering people to disrupt an industry through timeless Servant Leadership principles to make the world better. Companies, by and large, aren't very good at inspiring people to give their hearts, minds, and spirits to something big and audacious and meaningful. Movements are good at this.

When it comes to motivating people, movements outperform companies. Here's why:

In a company, the basis for exchange is transactional or contractual—a fair day's wage for a fair day's labor. In a movement, the exchange is voluntary and transformational—you give your gifts, talents, and time in exchange for an opportunity to do something heroic and meaningful, to make a difference.

In a company, you are an "asset" to be managed, a tool for production, a means to an end. In a movement, you are a partner in a cause, a "co-sojourner" if you will, fighting against some evil or ill in the world that you want to make right.

In a company, people are loyal to the firm and vice versa because they depend on each other economically. In a movement, people are loyal to each other because they share a commitment to a cause and a sense of belonging to something bigger.

National Life and its associates are in partnership with general agents, independent agents, and financial advisors.

You can't manage them like you would a direct reporting relationship in a company. Why would you want to? Most companies rely on rules, regulations, and thick, convoluted policy manuals to control people. Movements, by contrast, give people the freedom to operate within the vision, values, and norms defined by the cause.

Want to legislate passion, creativity, initiative, and accountability? **Good luck.**

At some point you will have to look in the mirror and ask, "How's that workin' for ya?"

Even in a tightly controlled organization people choose to give these gifts or not. Exhort them (with carrots or sticks) to try harder, do more, serve the customers, and stomp on the competitors all you want; it won't work. You may get compliance—but only for a while.

At National Life we want our culture to be as human as the human beings in it. We want people to bring their passion, creativity, initiative, and accountability to our cause for the long haul ... because they want to, not because they have to.

Our culture is as much the will of our people as it is the will of our executives. We all want to feel valued, add value, and live our values every day.

Sean Woodroffe
Senior Vice President
People Department

Although National Life University offers an extensive array of training programs and workshops designed to stretch, grow, and develop its people, there is one program that drives home the importance of opting in vs. buying in; it is called **Bringing Life to What We Do**.

The focus and purpose of this course is for employees to more fully understand how everyone adds value to the life of a policy (or not). Employees are able to think through how their gifts, talents, skills, and leadership impact the agents and, ultimately, the policy holder. Employees are encouraged to think of a story that is a good example of how their role connects to the bigger picture, how they Do Good, Be Good or Make Good in the spirit of delivering on a promise.

Saving a customer $800,000. Here is just one example of how this program inspired an employee to go above and beyond to Do Good for a customer.

A policy owner contacted National Life to make an ownership change on a non-qualified annuity. A customer service representative contacted the individual who held Power of Attorney (POA) to advise them about the taxable amount of the annuity because the ownership change would cost over $800,000. The customer service representative contacted the POA a number of times explaining the details and the ramifications of the ownership change. The POA finally understood and decided against the ownership change.

This employee's commitment to Do Good, Be Good, and Make Good saved the customer an unexpected and potentially outrageous tax expenditure.

Another highlight of the training involves an opportunity to "get real with an agent."

Get Real with an Agent is a conversation with a National Life agent who shares his or her own personal client experiences and explains how the employees of National Life are a critical link in supporting products and maintaining relationships with all policy holders.

These important conversations between agents and employees create a powerful dynamic, an insightful exchange, and a safe forum for asking questions. The dialogue also contributes to breaking down tribes/silos, growing networks, and increasing everyone's awareness of the importance of opting in, adding value, and bringing LIFE assurance to everything they do.

Sadly, we live in a world that uses people and loves things.

Unpacking the National Life story has us asking: "Why not create a movement that sees people not as assets to be managed, but rather as talented, impassioned, and gifted entrepreneurs to be enabled, empowered, and trusted to Do Good?

Why not create a community that loves and values people and uses things to enrich lives?"

What if we created a company that was as human as the human beings in it?

PART 8
WILL BUY FOR A CAUSE
PEOPLE DON'T BUY PRODUCTS
THEY BUY BETTER VERSIONS OF THEMSELVES

T his business truism can be interpreted from two perspectives. First, people buy products to increase convenience, improve their experience, and enrich their lives—essentially to create a better version of themselves.

LET'S ENRICH LIVES.

Apple created an entire ecosystem of products and services that have made our lives better. In healthcare alone, would Steve Jobs have even guessed that today there are more than 13,000 health apps available for download in Apple's App Store?

As its retail stores opened, Jobs told the people at Apple, "Your customers don't care about your products. Your customers dream of a happier and better life. Don't move products. Instead, enrich lives." People don't care about 1GB storage; they care about 1,000 songs in their pocket.

Like Apple, the people of National Life are extremely proud of their products and innovative financial solutions. But it's not enough to just push or pitch products. Imagine disrupting the industry with a game-changing product that solves a very real problem—that matters! That's radical.

IMAGINE A LIFE INSURANCE POLICY YOU DON'T' HAVE TO DIE TO USE. THAT'S RADICAL.

WHAT'S AT THE HEART OF YOUR INVESTING?

Imagine a life insurance policy you can use if chronic illness or serious injury disrupts your routine, your life *while you're living*. That's radical.

Imagine an annuity product you can draw income from in retirement…before you die. That's radical.

I DID SOME GOOD TODAY. GO ME!

The second interpretation of the headline above is that, when we serve others, when we do something to create a better world, we also create a better version of ourselves. We are enriched when we buy products that enrich lives from companies that are doing good.

MY PURCHASES ARE A STATEMENT ABOUT ME.

Blake Mycoskie, founder of TOMS Shoes, chose the name TOMS to signify "Shoes for Tomorrow" because with every pair of shoes you buy, the company donates a pair to a child in need. Mycoskie came up with the idea during a trip to Argentina where he noticed that many of the children he met didn't have shoes—a problem in developing countries where one of the leading causes of disease is soil-transmitted parasites that penetrate bare feet. He also learned that many of these children couldn't go to school if they didn't have shoes.

Now, why do people pay an average of $55 and as much as $100 for a pair of TOMS? The shoes are essentially stretched canvas glued to thin rubber soles. It's because every time we buy a pair of TOMS we feel a part of something bigger, a part of doing something good in the world. And when we look in the mirror we see a better version of ourselves.

A BETTER VERSION OF ME FEELS…WELL…BETTER!

People seek self-expression and self-identity through what they buy. What good parent or spouse doesn't feel responsible for protecting the financial well-being of their family?

HERE IS HOW THE PEOPLE OF NATIONAL LIFE SEE IT:

- Who, after investing in assurance today for peace of mind in the future…
- Who, after purchasing a product that has both death and living benefits…
- Who, after making their future more secure, can't look in the mirror and see a better version of themselves?

169

Life is a Journey
Jessica's Story

When Jessica, only 30 years old and a new mom, needed assurance it started with an unexpected call from her doctor. Jessica had breast cancer. One of her saving graces was the assurance she gained through her relationship with National Life.

We've been using it a lot. It has come to define National Life. So let's unpack that word ASSURANCE for a minute.

Assurance is a promise, pledge, oath, or bond we make to ourselves and others that offers security, inspires confidence, and creates a sense of certainty. Assurance removes doubt and lowers fear and anxiety. It guarantees that we will be there with the needed resources when something unscripted happens.

Assurance is a gift. And, who, after giving such a gift to the people they love and care about most, can't see a better version of themselves?

Ask customers like Jessica or Sharlene Nelson or go back in time and ask Rowland Allen what they see after buying a living benefits policy. Here's what you are going to hear:

WE SEE A BETTER VERSION OF OURSELVES!

Since May 2006, TOMS has given over 600,000 pairs of shoes to children in need. Check out the QR code below of their shoe distribution in Haiti.

WHY ARE WE DRAWN TO BRANDS WITH A CAUSE?

As explained by Blake Mycoskie, founder of TOMS, in a speech at the Dell Social Innovation, TOMS not only help us express our identity, they make us feel like we belong—to something bigger, more important than ourselves that, in turn, lends significance to who we are.

If you don't stand for something, you will fall for anything....

John Mellencamp

OUR BRAND
A PROMISE...AN EMOTIONAL CONNECTION

At the end of the day, your brand is not in your control. It's what your employees, partners, and customers say about you. But YOU can influence your brand.

FOR A BRAND TO STAND OUT IT HAS TO STAND FOR SOMETHING.

So you have to tell a compelling story about the cause for which you fight. That story must generate a real emotional response from your partners and customers. They have to see and know and feel that when they buy your products, they too are connected to something bigger, something good, and something enriching.

The durability and weightiness of your brand will be determined by how well you foster a meaningful, emotional relationship between your customers and the assurance in your promises.

> *Train people well enough so they can leave, treat them well enough so they don't want to.*
>
> *Richard Branson*

If people feel good about the decision and if they know they are connected to something good, they will refer over and over again. They will be loyal and they will want to share your story too. Below is a note from a loyal National Life policy holder:

> *Thank you to Ms. Argenti, she deserves it. You have a great associate and I believe your company chooses great employees like her that is why I am willing and want to spread the word about you. My husband has a HUGE family and thousands of friends. If you would like to send me business cards I will be more than happy to sing your praises and pass them around.*

AND THEY WILL HELP YOU SPREAD THE WORD.

Which means more people will want and trust you. More people will buy your products and your promise.

The movement will grow stronger, and with 16,000 advisors and more wanting in, you will enrich lives on a larger scale.

ARE YOU UP FOR IT?

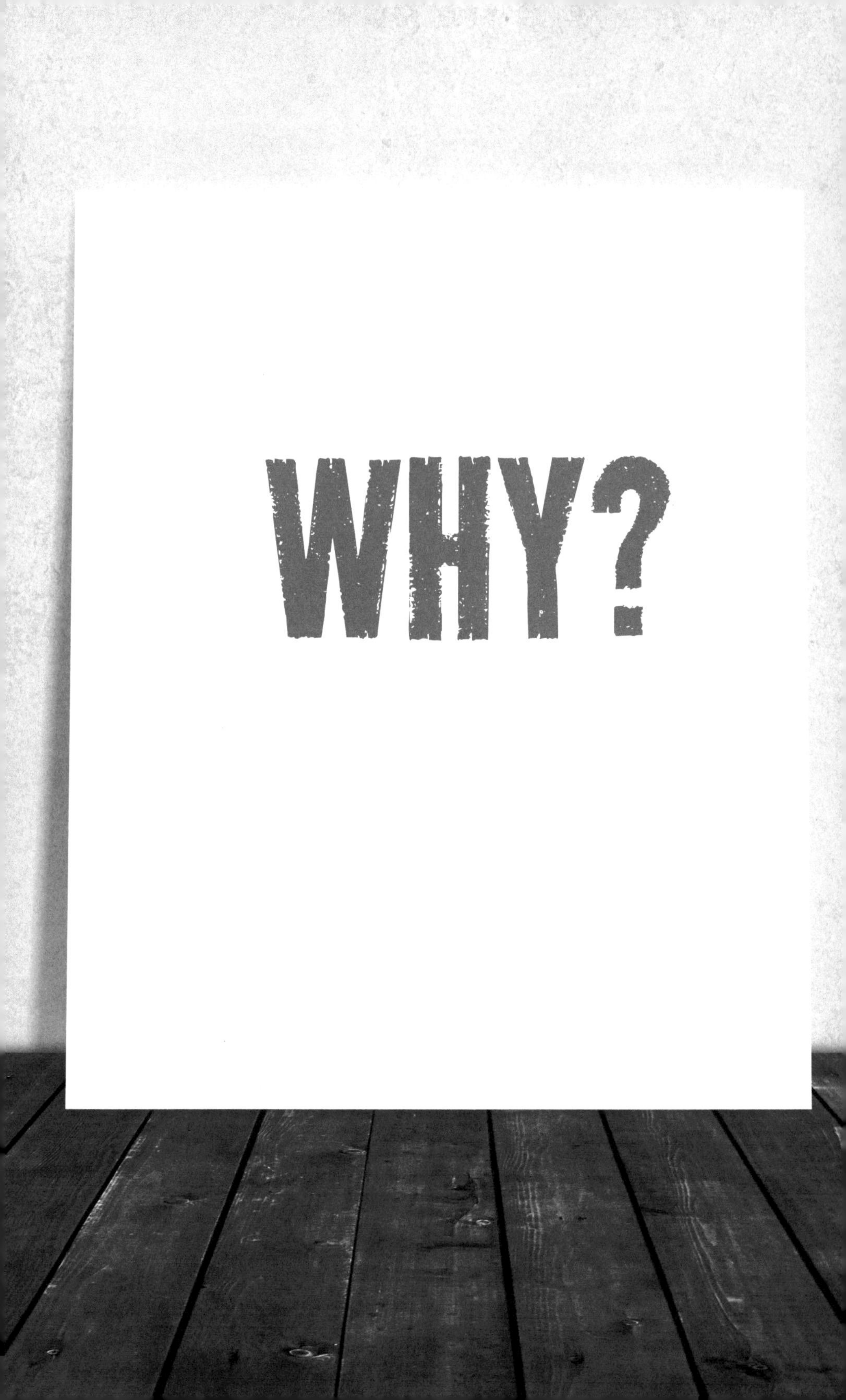
WHY?

PRODUCTS GIVE LIFE TO THE CAUSE

PEOPLE DON'T BUY WHAT YOU DO; THEY BUY WHY YOU DO IT.

WHY = THE REASON TO BUY.
WHAT = THE TANGIBLE PROOF OR EVIDENCE TO SUPPORT THAT REASON.

What happens when other companies come along and pitch similar products with similar features and benefits to yours? When that happens you end up in a commodity game competing on price, trying to differentiate yourselves based on incremental features and benefits.

But if you stay focused on WHY you are doing this, you will always be different because your products give life to something bigger that people will tap into. Your products give life to the cause.

When you sell WHY you do what you do, you are inviting people to join a movement that gives them an opportunity to express themselves. It gives them a platform to tell their story, to make a statement about who they are, what they believe, and what they stand for. Isn't this what we see in the stories of people whose lives have been changed by assurance democratized? It also gives them a sense of belonging, a place where they can join like-minded people who share the same concerns and aspirations. This is what people are buying.

WHY distinguishes Southwest Airlines from everyone else. It's not WHAT they do; it's WHY they do it that captures people's attention. There are a lot of companies that will sell you a seat and move you from point A to point B. But there's only one company that set out to fight for the little person. There's only one that initially got into business to democratize the skies. This is their WHY.

Make no mistake. Southwest's WHY informs their WHAT and HOW. If you truly have an egalitarian value system and exist to democratize the skies, then you don't nickel and dime customers by charging for bags just because everyone else does. But you do unleash the entrepreneurial spirit of your people to manage every penny out of the cost of doing business.

In many respects, Southwest is an assurance company too. They don't talk much about legroom, clean planes, and better service. They transcend the features and benefits debate by talking about the WHY. They tell you that they are a "Symbol of Freedom," giving you the freedom to "GO, SEE and DO" the things you dream about.

WHEN POTENTIAL CUSTOMERS BUMP INTO AGENTS WHAT SPILLS OUT IS THE WHY

WHO DOESN'T WANT MORE OF THAT?

It's one thing to stand on the sidelines and critique an industry for exploiting people. Many people think insurance companies do. You could probably create a movement around that alone. But it's quite another thing to use relevant, innovative products to fuel a bigger YES.

Like Southwest, the people of National Life see their products and services as a means to a bigger end, the tools with which they address the bigger WHY.

We suspect the reason their agents have been so successful when other companies are flat is that they aren't just hocking yet another insurance product with unique features. Rather, when potential customers bump into them, what spills out of their agents is the WHY:

> *... ensuring that families stay together and businesses and legacies continue*
>
> *... preserving the dignity and financial independence of seniors*
>
> *... helping people through illness and providing streams of income when they're needed most*
>
> *... creating a safe and secure haven in unpredictable times*
>
> *... giving newly-acquired friends peace of mind*

Ultimately, this is what the people of National Life are selling. And guess what? It resonates. The story almost sells itself.

Their promises (the WHAT) are cool, but what make the people in the field so successful is their passion for talking to customers about using those promises to build a better world for their families (the WHY).

PART 9
WHAT DIFFERENCE WILL YOU MAKE?
WHAT WILL YOU LEAVE BEHIND?

Extraordinary leaders will ask these questions:

ARE THOSE WHO ARE LEFT BEHIND IMPACTED AND MOVED TO CARRY ON MY WORK LONG AFTER I'VE LEFT THE SCENE?

ARE THOSE WHO FOLLOW ME LEARNING? GROWING? SERVING? EFFECTING CHANGE?

You may have heard about the Swedish chemist named Alfred who made a fortune by inventing some of the most powerful explosives of his time. He was a very smart businessman as well because he licensed his formula and sold it to governments and military installations all around world. In today's terms, he became a billionaire.

Then, a tragedy occurred. An explosion in one of Alfred's factories killed his brother. Mourning the loss, Alfred opened a French newspaper to read his brother's obituary. Unfortunately, the newspaper screwed it up and accidently printed an article about Alfred instead of his brother.

CAN YOU IMAGINE?

What would it be like to grieve the loss of a loved one, expecting to read their obituary, only to find it's about you?

The paper portrayed Alfred as a brilliant inventor of explosives and a man who made his fortune by enabling armies all over the globe to achieve new levels of mass destruction and mass annihilation.

WHAT WILL
YOUR LEGACY BE?

ALFRED WAS SHOCKED.

He couldn't bear to think that he would be remembered as a merchant of death and destruction. So he took his fortune and used it to establish a series of awards to be given to people who excel in their respective fields and benefit humanity by creating a better world.

As it turns out history remembers Alfred Nobel not for his formula for dynamite, but for the Nobel Prizes and what they represent.

Alfred had a unique and bizarre opportunity to see how he would be remembered. Few of us get that luxury.

NOW YOU WHAT IF WE TOLD YOU THAT YOU ONLY HAVE SIX MONTHS TO LIVE?

Would it change your sense of urgency? The way you spend your time? Your level of passion for doing meaningful work and living a life that matters?

NOW, THE TOUGHER QUESTION...WHAT MAKES ANY OF US THINK WE ARE GUARANTEED SIX MONTHS?

And when life is unscripted and the journey actually ends, the time to ask, "What is my legacy?" is NOT at the end of the journey; it's here, now, today!

SO, WHAT ABOUT YOU?

If a person lives and dies without anyone noticing, did that person really live? What kind of person do you wish to become by the time you die? What steps are you taking today?

THIS JOURNEY IS GOING TO END. IT COULD BE TOMORROW OR MANY, MANY YEARS FROM NOW.

When it does, here is what will happen. They are going to drop you in the ground, throw dirt on you, and then go back to the church or temple or synagogue and eat potato salad. And they will reminisce about you.

WHAT WOULD YOU LIKE THEM TO SAY?

"_____ was one of the most talented guys I knew. He could've transformed our entire industry with his creativity and novel ideas, but they wouldn't let him."

"_____ had the insights of ten people. Her ideas could've changed the world, but they wouldn't listen."

NICE EPITAPH? STIMULATING EULOGY?

We suspect the people of National Life know too well, there are no guarantees. An article in the Wall Street Journal stated that 70 percent of Americans are living paycheck-to-paycheck. Other industry data suggests there are approximately 1.2 million critical illnesses a year. And with these illnesses people also suffer a loss of income, sometimes temporary and sometimes long-term. Perhaps that's why 60 percent of bankruptcies are medically related.

If most of us are living paycheck-to-paycheck, we are in serious need of some guarantees.

EVEN THOUGH THERE ARE NO GUARANTEES, THERE IS ASSURANCE.

And when life is unscripted and the journey actually ends, the time to ask, "What is my legacy?" is NOT at the end of the journey; it's here, now, today!

AND THERE'S ONE MORE THING THAT'S GOING TO HAPPEN AFTER THEY DROP YOU IN THE GROUND.

WRITE YOUR OWN...
WHAT WOULD IT SAY?

At your burial site, they are going to place a tombstone with an inscription on it. Do you want it to say this?

Your Name
1965 - ___
Made Quota! Sold 3,122 policies!

That's not the way to measure a life.

Based upon all that we have learned about their journey from relevance to prominence, we believe the people of National Life and their partners will look back on their time and their commitment to assurance and say this:

> *I was a part of a company. Not just any company, but a company that protects people from heartbreaking, unexpected circumstances and the financial ruin that can follow.*
>
> *Our company enriches businesses, homes, and lives. We are grounded in timeless Servant Leadership principles and we gain inspiration from the heroes of our past.*
>
> *We are a movement of like-minded people who Do Good, Be Good and Make Good on our promises and bring peace of mind to all we serve.*
>
> *We make the world better by democratizing life assurance so your dreams, hopes, dignity, and financial independence can prevail.*

NOT BAD, EH?

Mehran Assadi and the people of National Life provide yet another powerful example of what happens when a company defines itself in terms of a cause and sees itself as not just a company but a movement and a crusade.

SO WHAT ABOUT YOU?...IF YOU DISAPPEARED TOMORROW, WOULD YOU BE MISSED?

OR WOULD THE WORLD JUST BE LESS CROWDED?

CAUSE FUELS
THE FIRES
OF COURAGE
AND
PERSEVERANCE

ONE LAST THING

So ask yourself: *Do I want to be part of a business that's engaged in a movement?*

This isn't just a philosophical question; it is foundational to building an engaging culture and growing your business. Here's why:

CAUSE ANIMATES CULTURE.

Like breathing pure oxygen after a rigorous climb, a heroic cause brings vitality and life to an organization. It creates excitement. Hearts are moved and minds are activated. Imaginations run at full bore. New ideas abound. People are more willing to take risks and be accountable for decisions that support the cause.

Policies and practices that aren't aligned with the cause are challenged. Petty preoccupations submerge in the wake of a bigger, more exciting "YES!" Language intensifies, confidence grows, and convictions become stronger—people naturally want to "opt-in."

CAUSE UNLEASHES COMMITMENT, ENERGY, AND CREATIVITY.

A cause raises aspirations and the belief that we CAN, indeed, effect change, way more than if we were just showing up to a job. If this doesn't capture your attention, enlist, and elevate you, no worries. It means you might be happier somewhere else. On the other hand, if your heart and mind are moved by the cause, if you get a shot of adrenaline from bringing assurance—living benefits, protection, peace of mind, and financial freedom to others, you're in the right place and you're in good company at National Life.

CAUSE FUELS THE FIRES OF COURAGE AND PERSEVERANCE.

Transforming a culture is difficult. National Life has been committed to a One Company, One Culture transformation for over ten years. Launching a movement is even more difficult. Neither follows a nice, neat, linear path. There are false starts and missteps along the way. Both require the ability to bounce back—over and over again. By definition, disrupting the status quo is about confronting unprecedented challenges in uncharted territory. That's messy!

Where do you find the "stick-to-itiveness" to hang in there when darkness sets in, the terrain gets rough, and the way is uncertain?

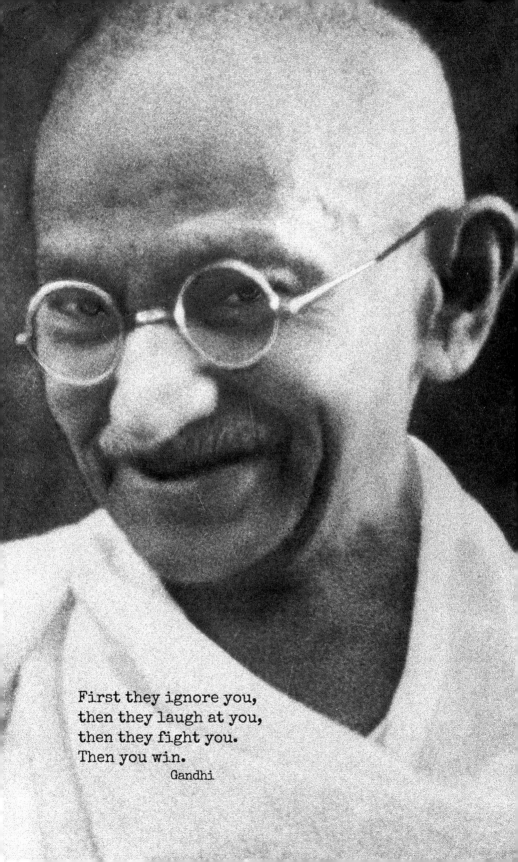

First they ignore you,
then they laugh at you,
then they fight you.
Then you win.
                    Gandhi

Change is never easy. As National Life develops new unconventional products and fresh, innovative ways of serving customers, and as it continues to cascade the One Company, One Culture, One Cause message, it will inevitably run up against resistance.

When resistance occurs, when they ignore, laugh, even fight against the culture, the cause, or the Servant Leadership tenets, what will the people of National Life do?

Give in? Give up? Check out? Or stand strong in the values and principles that have built this movement for more than 167 years?

The people of National Life should find their own assurance in knowing they are the secret sauce. **Products can be copied and investments can be duplicated, but HOW and WHY they deliver on the promises is what makes National Life different**—they bring LOVE to each promise delivered.

So, if resistance strikes and darkness follows, lean into the message in Passenger's song, "Scare Away the Darkness" and "Love without fear in your heart."

Well, sing, sing at the top of your voice,
Love without fear in your heart.
Feel, feel like you still have a choice
If we all light up we can scare away the dark

We wish our weekdays away
Spend our weekends in bed
Drink ourselves stupid
And work ourselves dead
And all just because that's what mom and dad said we should do

We should run through the forest
We should swim in the streams
We should laugh, we should cry,
We should love, we should dream
We should stare at the stars and not just the screens
You should hear what I'm saying and know what it means

To sing, sing at the top of your voice,
Love without fear in your heart.
Feel, feel like you still have a choice
If we all light up we can scare away the dark

Well, we wish we were happier, thinner and fitter,
We wish we weren't losers and liars and quitters
We want something more not just nasty and bitter
We want something real not just hash tags and Twitter

It's the meaning of life and it's streamed live on YouTube
But I bet Gangnam Style will still get more views
We're scared of drowning, flying and shooters
But we're all slowly dying in front of flippin computers

So sing, sing at the top of your voice,
Oh, love without fear in your heart.
Can you feel, feel like you still have a choice
If we all light up we can scare away the dark

When the cause is heroic, the achievements of the movement will outlive you. You will be able to look back on your life and work and know that you made a lasting contribution that, without you, would not exist.

When the cause is deeply inspiring, it has the potential to differentiate any business in a sea of sameness. Cause and culture will draw the right people in, people with fire in their belly.

The people of National Life are grounded in timeless principles—love and friendship, assuring the American Dream and making good on a promise. They live these principles out loud daily because the noble, heroic cause for which they fight depends on it. They are not just a company; they are a movement that is growing stronger one relationship at a time.

This is their legacy.

JACKIE AND KEVIN FREIBERG

Are bestselling authors and founders of the San Diego Consulting Group Inc. The Freibergs are dedicated to helping leaders create Best Places where the Best People can do their Best Work to make the world Better. Both have Ph.D.'s and teach part-time at the University of San Diego, School of Leadership and Education Sciences.

In their international bestseller *NUTS! Southwest Airlines' Crazy Recipe for Business and Personal Success,* Kevin and Jackie uncovered the strategies that created the greatest success story in the history of commercial aviation. NUTS! was followed by:

GUTS! Companies that Blow the Doors Off Business-as-usual;
BOOM! 7 Choices for Blowing the Doors Off Business-as-usual;

NANOVATION: How a Little Car Can Teach the World to Think Big, the inside story of one of the greatest innovations in the auto industry since the Model-T. It's also a roadmap for expanding your capacity to innovate and making innovation part of your cultural DNA; and

DO SOMETHING NOW, three simple words that will change your organization—change your life. The scarcest resource in organizations right now is not money, talent, ideas or power; it's people who DO, people who add value and get things done. DSN inspires Dreamers to become Doers. Everyone wants to add value and this book shows you how.

BE A PERSON OF IMPACT: 12 Strategies to be the CEO of Your Future. This book is an unapologetic kick in the butt to proactively manage your brand and reputation. POI will challenge you to reimagine, rethink, refresh and even completely reengineer your brand. Why? Because your brand is in your control. If you want to be indispensable, stand-out as the best in your business and lead others to do the same this book will show you how.

The Freibergs speak on **leadership**, **innovation** and **change** all over the world. They have a global practice including firms in Europe, Japan, South Africa, India, Central and South America, as well as companies throughout the United States and Canada.

To book Jackie or Kevin for an event or to reach out in general, email kevinandjackie@freibergs.com or call 619-624-9691.

COVER ATTRIBUTION

DEAR WORLD

A business, art and social experiment designed to change the world one message-on-skin portrait at a time. Visit DEAR WORLD and be inspired by their photo gallery of loss, struggle, fear, hope, joy and... love. http://www.dearworld.me/story/

ENVIRONMENTAL IMPACT

Printing: Printed by Villanti Printers, Inc., environmentally certified to the Forest Stewardship Council® Standards. Manufactured using 100% Green-E® Certified Renewable Energy.

Paper: Printed on New Leaf Reincarnation Silk 120-lb. cover and New Leaf Ingenuity 80-lb. text. This paper is derived from 100% postconsumer recycled fiber, manufactured using 100% Green-E® Certified Renewable Energy and is certified through Bureau Veritas to the Forest Stewardship Council Standards.

Savings derived from using postconsumer recycled fiber in lieu of virgin fiber*:

| 105 trees not cut down | 3,302 lbs. solid waste not generated | 9,768 lbs. atmospheric emmisions not generated | 49,339 gallons water/wastewater flow saved |

*Calculated using the New Leaf Paper EcoAudit Calculator.

RECYCLED
Paper made from recycled material
FSC
www.fsc.org   FSC® C013435

Green-e

Paper Manufactured and Printed Using 100% Certified Renewable Electricity
TN#: 10-5005-1079